NINE HORRIBLE DAYS

The story of the kidnap of Archbishop Kattey

———————●———————

Ignatius Crosby Ogboru Kattey DD

PARTRIDGE

Library of Congress Control Number: 2019920092
ISBN: Hardcover   978-1-5437-5458-2
                Softcover   978-1-5437-5457-5
                eBook   978-1-5437-5456-8

Print information available on the last page.

To order additional copies of this book, contact
Toll Free 800 101 2657 (Singapore)
Toll Free 1 800 81 7340 (Malaysia)
orders.singapore@partridgepublishing.co

www.partridgepublishing.com/singapore

CONTENTS

PREFACE

Archbishop Ignatius Kattey, Archbishop of Niger Delta and Bishop of Niger Delta North in Nigeria, has written a remarkable book about his violent kidnap in September 2013. He sets the scene by describing the proceedings of the Provincial Council held at the Cathedral Church of All Saints, Uyo, in the Diocese of Uyo, on Wednesday, 4 September, that year. From there, he and his small party went on to Yenagoa for another event before returning home. Quite apart from the picture that this gives of an active and thriving Anglican diocese, it serves to illustrate the normality of the Archbishop's situation immediately—prayerfully and conscientiously overseeing his flock—prior to the violent events which followed. Just a few days later, on their way to another engagement, he and his wife were pulled menacingly from their car by kidnappers, who subsequently demanded a ransom.

In this book, he describes what followed in graphic detail. The ordeal which both he and his wife, Beatrice, underwent at the hands of clearly determined and irresponsible assailants is hard to read, but throughout it, their faith in Jesus Christ shines through, in spite of his physical sufferings in the hands of desperate men, he is able to see his kidnappers as individual human beings, themselves caught up in complex life situations. Whilst naturally anxious that justice should be done, he remains free from any thoughts of vengeance. In its own way, this is a remarkable piece of Christian testimony which combines a hard-headed and realistic account of others' criminal behaviour with a refusal to waver from a deep-seated faith in the power and love of God to transcend human frailty. Archbishop Kattey makes frequent references in his book to the Old Testament accounts of God's justice, set against the weakness and waywardness of the human condition. The strength and depth of his faith will serve as an example to many.

Most Reverend & Right Honourable Justin Welby
Archbishop of Canterbury, Primate of All England and Metropolitan

FOREWORD

Archbishop Ignatius Kattey's kidnap story is chilling and is an experience that should not be wished for even an enemy. The news of his kidnap was all over the world, and prayers were offered for his release.

What made his kidnap more spectacular was that he was unable to participate in the biannual Standing Committee meeting of the Church of Nigeria (Anglican Communion), which took place in his domain, the Province of Niger Delta. He was kidnapped three days to the meeting.

Saint Ignatius, as I call him, is deeply spiritual. As Primate of All Nigeria, I presided over his consecration (and over his election during my brief period as Dean of the Church of Nigeria). He sometimes accompanied me in my Evangelism travels, and I think I am in an advantaged position to testify about his spirituality. St. Ignatius excelled in Missions and Evangelism.

Even in his captivity, he was still communicating with God as if he were a free man, from his testimony in the book.

This reminds us of our Patriarch Joseph, who was put in prison for a crime he did not commit: 'Then Joseph's master took him and put him into prison . . . But the LORD was with Joseph and showed him mercy' (Genesis 39:20–21).

This book has an account of his nine days in the hands of unwanted friends. The idea of being in the midst of people he had never met before—hostile people—was torturous enough to make him doubt God, but Archbishop Kattey, in his book, held on to his faith in God. He went on to have his 'Quiet Time' or 'Morning Devotion', a practice he imbibed from the Scripture Union ministry, where he said he was converted. He kept on praying and meditating on the Word of God.

Saint Ignatius forgave his captors (those who made him go through this ordeal) at the time of his release, and this he affirmed in the court of law when he was persuaded to testify.

I recommend this book for all.

Archbishop Peter J. Akinola
Former Primate and Metropolitan, Church of Nigeria (Anglican Communion)

ACKNOWLEDGEMENTS

This is a very difficult task for a book of this nature. It is necessary to first of all acknowledge the world—Christians, Muslims, and those of other faith who by their prayers, visitation, etc. showed great concern during and after our ordeal. Some of them I have never met in life and may never meet.

A man from Australia met me in Jerusalem and took a photograph with Beatrice and me. He said he would show it to his son, who, together with the family, prayed for us. When we were released, the son asked, 'Daddy, can we now stop fasting since the Archbishop has been released?' Even the press was not left out.

I am grateful to all my immediate office staff: Sir Chidi Adiele; Sir Barr; Emeka Ichoku; Dame Tonye Dombraye; Sir O. C. Chukwu; Dame Okechukwu Owhonda; Sir Joseph Oriji; Mr Humphrey Amadi; Sister Uchenna Agbazue; Sister Patience Chinda; Rev. Canon Manasseh Y. Oguru; Ven. David Eguare; Mrs Joy Olungwe; Rev. Canon Samuel Chujor; Rev. Canon (now Venerable) Romauld Foko; Rev. Canon Udoamaka Nehemiah; Rev. Gideon Otuawaji; Rev. Canon (now Venerable) Ugochukwu Okpala; Rev. Emmanuel Makele; Ven. John Adubasim; Ven. Chimela Samuel; Ven. Ben Enwuchola, who was the head of Nigerian Chaplaincy in UK at the time of my kidnap; Sir Ngozi and Dame Kate Abu; Sir and Lady Nnamdi Udensi; Sir and Lady Obianko Elechi; the chief security adviser for the Province of Niger Delta and Diocese of Niger Delta North, Sir Chief Alexander Orakwue; Ven. Collins and Mrs Peace Asonye; Mrs Juliet Akpan; Mr Friday Korsi; Mr Eric Olomi; Mr Ibalafaa Peters; Rev. Canon Olungwe and wife Stella; clergy and wives of Diocese of Niger Delta North and the Province of Niger Delta; and all the faithful of the Diocese of Niger Delta North and Province of Niger Delta.

Mrs Mabel Peters did all the typing and retyping. She was very useful, and I am very grateful to her.

I wish to thank all the publishers and editors who permitted me to use their materials. Some of them are:

- East African Centre for Law and Justice—based in Nairobi, Kenya
- *The Church Times* newspaper—London
- Naija Gist News
- *P.M. News*, published by Independent Communications Network
- *African Examiner*—Oludare Fashe
- Radio Premier
- Bishop David Hamid—Eurobishop
- *Church Newspaper*—Colin Blakely
- *Church Times*—Paul Handley
- Lambeth Palace Press—Galvin Drake
- News Ghana 101
- *Daily Post*

My immediate family and friends, I acknowledge you all.

- Ven. Sullivan and Barr. Margaret Odike
- Rev. Canon Amos and Mrs Blessing Osaromkpe
- Mr Kelly Ejiro and Mrs Goodness Dibofun
- Dr Kattey and Mrs Sandra Kattey

- Mr Steve and Mrs Jane Amugo
- Mr Barny Ebere and Mrs Josephine Nwagbo
- Mr Immanuel Kattey
- Miss Beatrice (Jnr) Goada Gbute-Kattey

There are people difficult not to acknowledge, my beloved friends who are like blood brothers: Mr Godwin and Mrs Victoria Chu, Sir Dr Gabriel and Dame Fyne Ngegwe.

Our prayer partners at various times and stages in life include Brother Goya Ejire (who had gone to be with the Lord very early in life); Mr (now Rev. Canon) Amos Osaromkpe (married to Blessing); Mrs Charity Chujor (wife of Dr Chujor S. N. Chujor); Evangelist Charity Amasi-Gomba; Brother (now Professor) Zaccheus Oyedokun of Namibia University of Science and Technology in Windhoek; Rev. Moses Rahaman Popoola of the New Testament Christian Mission in Ilorin, Nigeria; my brethren Rev. and Mrs Loveday Nwafor; Pastor and Mrs Olaka N. Olaka; Rev. and Rev. Mrs Friday O. Osaronwolu; and Pastor and Mrs Friday Laleobe.

I also acknowledge my siblings: Sir Joseph and Lady Charity Kattey, Madam Comfort Ngede and husband Emmanuel, Archbishop Moses Olaka and Mrs Ntobari Kattey, Sir Walter Gbute and Lady Abigail Kattey, Elder Godsend Giokabari and wife Innocenta, and Bishop Jonathan Ruhumiliza and wife Asenath.

INTRODUCTION

This book is an autobiographical testimony of an Archbishop, doctor, and engineer, Ignatius Kattey, presented with Christian homilies, extracts of major speeches, and theological/spiritual viewpoints. It documents God's gracious call, ministry, impact, and deliverance of this man of God and his dearly beloved and godly wife, Beatrice, during their encounter with kidnappers, followed by days the husband spent in captivity in the 'den of lions'. When the Bishop of Niger Delta North, Archbishop of Niger Delta Province, and later Dean of the Church of Nigeria (Anglican Communion) was abducted, the entire nation and beyond were alarmed and in prayers. Massive security efforts were deployed, yet according to the author, it was God's mercy and grace that sustained him during the gruesome and humiliating torture and environmental hazards until he was released and reunited with his family and diocese. The striking elements of this man of God in all these experiences are his unwavering faith in God's miraculous intervention and protection of His anointed ones. His readiness to forgive his captors when they were eventually brought to face justice and the calamity that befell his betrayers, conspirators, and perpetrators prove the sacrosanct privilege of God's genuine ministers. 'Many indeed are the afflictions of the righteous, but the Lord delivers him from them all.'

Behind Archbishop Kattey's successful journey of life and ministry has been his faithful and devoted wife, Beatrice, a woman of strong faith, passionate love of God, gentle mien, and fervent prayer. The Kattey children proved their mettle as godly seeds and strong towers under the shepherding of their father, the Episcopes. He and his dear wife are a couple completely devoted to the service of God and prayer. Their core passions are global missions and churchmanship; these they fulfilled through decades of priesthood and episcopate. Remarkable miracles have been wrought through the ministry of Archbishop Kattey, including raising the dead! They and members of their family have encountered God's supernatural defence from diabolical forces on several occasions.

This book is richly enriched by many biblical texts, preaching, and charges presented in a broader evangelistic approach. Complementing biblical stories and precepts are numerous stories of people in Nigeria and other parts of the world whose life experiences are cited as warnings to others on how to live aright. This book is a 'pulpit' that preaches extempore to readers and prays for them at every needful point of the exposition, admonition, and testimony; this style gives the book much life and energy. In retirement, Archbishop Ignatius Kattey's publication herein continues a new dimension of his unending mission to the world.

I strongly commend this book to all genuine seekers of the truth of the gospel—Christians who trust in God's power to deliver to the uttermost and people for whom God is a succour of faith in these trying times of wanton insecurity of people in Nigeria and the world at large.

Rt Rev. Prof. Dapo F. Asaju
Professor of Theology,
Bishop Theologian of Church of Nigeria, and
Vice Chancellor of Ajayi Crowther University, Oyo, Nigeria

COMMENTS

- My husband, Crosby, and I were kidnapped together. At the first 'forest-stop' of the kidnappers, when we were seated, he asked for my release. Though I protested vehemently, my husband insisted, and I was released. That was at about 1.30 a.m. They asked me to go back to where our car was abandoned, about two or three kilometres away. On my going back in that dark forest, I felt some angelic presence, as if many persons were walking with me until I got to my destination. All I can say is this: God exists, and He cares. The rest of the story is about my husband's experience during the kidnap.

  Mrs Beatrice Goada Kattey

- The awesome power of God is always demonstrated in the lives of His children. No man born of a woman nor powers from the pit of hell can harm a genuine child of God. This book is a must-read for every child of God and, in fact, anyone who wants to understand the workings of God's power over the devil at all times and even anyone who is still in doubt about God's power to intervene in the affairs of man.

  Rt Rev. Wisdom Ihunwo
  Bishop, Diocese of Niger Delta North,
  Church of Nigeria (Anglican Communion)

- This book talks about the awesomeness of God Almighty. It shows that the author truly knows the God he serves, and is proud to make his God known to the world. The kidnap story is one that shows that God is an all-knowing God. Nothing happens by accident with him. He sees the end from the beginning. God desires true worship from His children.

Barrister (Mrs) Margaret Sullivan-Odike

- On the night of 6 September 2013, I received a call that my parents had been kidnapped. My mum was released a few hours later, but my dad spent nine days in the kidnappers' den. Those days were long and were filled with anxiety and palpable tension. It seemed like the plot of a horror or action movie. This book captures some of the events leading up to the kidnap and the activities that took place while he was being held by the kidnappers. By the special grace of God, our dad was released unhurt. As our God shut up the mouth of the lions who were with Daniel, so he was with His servant, our dad. In all this, we are persuaded that nothing can separate us from the love of God. He that keeps watch over us neither slumbers nor sleeps.

Dr Kattey Amos Kattey

- This is a spectacular account of God's power, protection, and deliverance of the real-life experience of His anointed servant, Archbishop Ignatius Kattey, from the hands of kidnappers. In the midst of wicked, destructive human agents of the forces of darkness, the Lord divinely preserved and set free His servant who is being mightily and fruitfully used by him. Perhaps the worlds of evil were angry and bitter at the focused, victorious, and triumphant ministry of this humble but 'dangerous' servant of God.

This unbelievable yet real experience of deliverance confirms God's Word that 'the snare is broken, and we are escaped' (Psalm 124:7). God has also demonstrated the truthfulness of His word, 'For the LORD is with me as the mighty terrible One, therefore, all my persecutors shall stumble . . . will not prevail . . . will be greatly ashamed . . . will not prosper' (Jeremiah 20:11). God will do this for and in the lives of all those who sincerely and committedly honour and serve Him. Revealed in this book is God's ultimate and unchallenged power, demonstrated over evil and heartless kidnappers. Yes, He is the unchallengeable God, the God of Archbishop Kattey! To God alone be the glory, honour, and praise. Amen in Jesus's name.

Solomon Olorundare
Professor of Science
University of Ilorin, Nigeria

- There is no doubt that Archbishop Kattey is a giant prayer warrior who puts all his trust in God alone. After being abducted for nine days, he was released unhurt and healthy. Archbishop Kattey strongly believes that God answers prayers. He was abducted for nine days and released unhurt. What a miracle. For me, he is a giant prayer warrior of our time who puts all his trust in God alone.

  Archbishop Kattey is indeed a genuine servant of God. He was abducted in the forest for nine days and was released unhurt because he prayed throughout his ordeal.

  Sir Chief Polycarp Ndounteng
  Managing Director/CEO
  Panef Integrated Services Ltd
  Port Harcourt

- When my mentor and father, the Archbishop, was kidnapped, we rushed to his house, and people were praying and weeping. I stopped the prayer (crying) and took authority. That was what was needed.

A friend called me from Lagos and said that some boys who had knowledge of the kidnapping in the community threatened that the Archbishop would be killed within two days.

I rather called for prayer of God's mercy and forgiveness on the kidnappers. And when my father was released, he too forgave them.

Kidnappers need mercy and forgiveness, not a curse Perhaps this is the main theme of this book—forgiveness.

Archbishop Moses Olaka Kattey, PhD, JP
General Overseer, Commonwealth Covenant Church International

• The engaging story of the kidnap and eventual release of Archbishop Ignatius Kattey has two underlying themes. The first is that there is always a consequence, in this world and in eternity, for any action or position we take in life. The genuine and determined effort of the Government of Rivers State and all security agencies in Nigeria to secure his release unhurt, the spontaneous prayer cells that arose throughout Nigeria and the rest of the Christian world to intercede with the God of heaven for his safety and release, and the eventual judgement of the mastermind of the kidnap by the God of heaven are a direct consequence of the quality of life Archbishop Kattey has led through the help of the triune God. With this understanding, men ought always to weigh all their actions and positions, knowing full well that they are not in a position to influence the consequences once the action and position are taken.

I am privileged to have been a friend, co-worker in the Lord's vineyard, and prayer partner of Archbishop Ignatius

Kattey for a period of over forty-five years, starting from our undergraduate days in the university to date. The second underlying theme in the kidnap story, which requires some highlight, is the subject of sanctification or holy living. Archbishop Ignatius Kattey gave his life to Christ through the ministry of the Scripture Union, which also inculcated in him the practice of daily study and meditation on the Word of God, the Bible. The emphasis on sanctification and holy living we received, separately in our growing-up days, through the ministry of the Apostolic Faith Church. There could never be a God of Kattey who raises the dead and does all other miracles in the name of Jesus Christ outside the subject of holy living. Daniel and his friends were spared the horrors of the lion's den because 'Daniel purposed in his heart that he will not defile himself with the portion of the king's meat' (Daniel 1:8). We must never lose sight of the scriptures, which says, 'And holiness without which no man shall see the Lord' (Hebrews 12:14).

Engr B. U. Bassey
Elder of the Presbyterian Church of Niger and Practising Civil Engineer

- The truth of the kidnap of the then Dean of the Church of Nigeria (Anglican Communion), the Most Reverend (Dr) Ignatius C. O. Kattey, JP, and his wife, Mrs Beatrice G. Kattey, JP, has been well summarily reported in the 2014 Nigeria national diary as the major national event of 6 September 2013: 'Dare devil kidnappers this night defiled God's Order which says "Touch not my anointed and do them no harm" as most Reverend Ignatius Kattey, Anglican Archbishop of the Niger Delta Province also Lord Bishop of Niger Delta North Diocese, and his wife Beatrice were kidnapped at Aleto-Eleme, the Bishop's hometown near Port Harcourt, Rivers State.'

At that time, we were the Archdeacon in charge of the Eleme Archdeaconry. The news came to us as the rudest shock of our ecclesiastical experience. The development precipitated the worst frustrations, multidimensional prayers, all kinds of meetings, uncontrolled media reactions nationally and internationally, mocking, lamentations, and the question 'Oh, where is God?' Though his wife was released a few hours later that night, the Archbishop was in the forest, in the custody of the abductors for nine nights, while prayers, protest processions roadblocks, press conferences, Internet communications, etc. were going on.

The Almighty God proved that He is God Almighty; on the night of Saturday, 15 September 2013, the Archbishop was freed. To God be the glory, who answered us and removed the disgraceful mocking from us. On his release, the Archbishop advocated for forgiveness for the kidnappers. We hoped the powers that be would listen. We celebrated his freedom with a diocesan thanksgiving service at the Holy Trinity Anglican Church in Nchia-Eleme.

Ven. Dr Israel O. Omosioni, JP
Archdeacon, Eleme Archdeaconry, 2013
Diocese of Niger Delta North, Church of Nigeria (Anglican Communion)

- Archbishop Kattey has written a faith-inspiring book. The book is a story of reciprocal love—of a man who sincerely loves God, who deeply loves him. You will cry, pray, praise, and fall in love with God in an authentic way as you read this book. This book is a gift to the current and next generation of people.

Mr Ben and Dr Grace Ukasoanya
Winnipeg, Canada

PROLOGUE

Make a joyful noise unto God, all ye lands.

Sing forth the honour of His name: make His praise glorious.

Say unto God, how terrible art Thou in Thy works! Through the greatness of Thy power shall thine enemies submit themselves unto Thee.

All the earth shall worship Thee, and shall sing unto Thee, they shall sing to Thy name.

Come and see the works of God: He is terrible in His doing toward the children of men.

He turned the sea into dry land: they went through the flood on foot: there did we rejoice in Him.

He ruleth by His power for ever: His eyes behold the nations: let not the rebellious exalt themselves.

O bless our God, ye people and make the voice of His praise to be heard

Which holdeth our soul in life, and suffereth not our feet to be moved.

For Thou, O God, hast proved us: Thou hast tried us, as silver is tried.

Thou broughtest us into the net; Thou laidst affliction upon our loins.

Thou hast caused men to ride over our heads, we went through fire and through water: but Thou broughtest us out into a wealthy place.

I will go into thy house with burnt offering: I will pay Thee my vows.

Which my lips have uttered, and my mouth hath spoken, when I was in trouble.

I will offer unto Thee burnt sacrifices of fatlings, with the incense of rams; I will offer bullocks with goats.

Come and hear, all ye that fear God, and I will declare what He hath done for my soul.

I cried unto Him with my mouth, and He was extolled with my tongue.

If I regard iniquity in my heart, the Lord will not hear me.

But verily God hath heard me; He hath attended to the voice of my prayer.

Blessed be God, which hath not turned away my
prayer, nor His mercy from me. (Psalm 66)

In the course of our joint morning prayers, I read this psalm with
my wife, Beatrice, and she suggested it should be used for our
thanksgiving. I readily agreed.

Days Before

As Archbishop of the Ecclesiastical Province of Niger Delta of
the Church of Nigeria (Anglican Communion), I scheduled our
Provincial Council meeting for Tuesday and Wednesday, 3 and 4
September 2013.

As our Anglican tradition demands, I had to be at Uyo on Monday, 2
September, as a speaker for a revival programme on Monday night,
Tuesday, and Wednesday—the 2nd, 3rd, and 4th, respectively—and
had to return on Thursday, the 5th. On 3 September, the Bishops
and wives met separately, and the 4th was the main Provincial
Council meeting. The Bishop of Uyo, the late Rt Rev. Isaac Orama,
was ill at the time, and the wife was not present at the provincial
meeting which he was hosting. To everybody's surprise, the faithful
in Uyo did very well to take care of the delegates of the Provincial
Council despite the fact that the Bishop and his wife were absent,
and this we commended.

The revival meeting was power packed, and it will help us
understand what will come later if the revival crusade messages
are reproduced as below.

DAY 1

Theme: 'The LORD, He is God, the LORD, He is God' (1 Kings 18:39).

'The LORD, He is God, the LORD, He is God.' Note that this was exclaimed twice. Apparently, the contest on Mount Carmel had proved that the God of Elijah that manifested by fire to consume the sacrifice (verse 38) is the Lord indeed. The LORD is not the small *lord* but the bold-lettered *LORD*, which means 'Jehovah'. This LORD is master. The living LORD is Jehovah Yahweh; He is God. Anything that people devote themselves to worshipping is a god. The president can be your god. Your job can be your god. Some people make images and put those images in their houses. Those images are their gods. But don't forget what Jehovah God says: 'I am the LORD your God. Thou shall not have any other gods before me [apart from me].'

Exodus 20:1–5 is a succinct explication of His reserved and exclusive personality:

I am the LORD your God who brought you out of the land of Egypt Out of the house of bondage. You shall have no other gods but me. You shall not make for yourselves, a carved image of any likeness of anything that is in heaven above or that is in the earth beneath or that is in the water under the earth. You shall not bow down to them nor serve them. For, I the LORD Jehovah your God am a jealous God, visiting the iniquity of the fathers upon the children to the third and fourth generation of those who hate Me. But showing mercy to thousands, to those who love Me and keep My commandments.

When Moses was to be wrapped with the presence of God in Exodus 33:34, he said, 'God show me Your face. I want to see Your face.'

Moses was a very daring man, very daring, a stammerer, but the Bible says he was the humblest man, the meekest man who ever lived on earth. Moses's own brother Aaron and his nanny sister, Miriam, both rebelled against Moses. They were older than Moses, of course. It must be noted that it was Miriam who was given the task of watching over baby Moses by the waterside before he was picked up by the daughter of Pharoah. It was Miriam who recommended their mother to take care of baby Moses.

Numbers 12:1–16 states,

> [1] And Miriam and Aaron spake against Moses because of the Ethiopian woman whom he had married: for he had married an Ethiopian woman

[2] And they said, Hath the Lord indeed spoken only by Moses? Hath He not spoken also by us? And the Lord heard it.

[3] (Now the man Moses was very meek, above all the men which were upon the face of the earth.)

[4] And the Lord spake suddenly unto Moses, and unto Aaron, and unto Miriam, Come out ye three unto the tabernacle of the congregation. And they came out.

[5] And the Lord came down in the pillar of cloud, and stood in the door of the tabernacle, and called Aaron and Miriam: and they both came forth.

[6] And He said, Hear now My words: If there be a prophet among you, I the Lord will make Myself known unto him in a vision, and will speak unto him in a dream.

[7] My servant Moses is not so, who is faithful in all Mine house.

[8] With him will I speak mouth to mouth, even apparently, and not in dark speeches; and the similitude of the Lord shall he behold: wherefore then were ye not afraid to speak against My servant Moses?

[9] And the anger of the Lord was kindled against them; and He departed.

[10] And the cloud departed from off the tabernacle; and, behold, Miriam became leprous, white as

snow: and Aaron looked upon Miriam, and, behold, she was leprous.

[11] And Aaron said unto Moses, Alas, my lord, I beseech thee, lay not the sin upon us, wherein we have done foolishly, and wherein we have sinned.

[12] Let her not be as one dead, of whom the flesh is half consumed when he cometh out of his mother's womb.

[13] And Moses cried unto the Lord, saying, Heal her now, O God, I beseech Thee.

[14] And the Lord said unto Moses, If her father had but spit in her face, should she not be ashamed seven days? let her be shut out from the camp seven days, and after that let her be received in again.

[15] And Miriam was shut out from the camp seven days: and the people journeyed not till Miriam was brought in again.

[16] And afterward the people removed from Hazeroth, and pitched in the wilderness of Paran.

It is instructive to hear God Almighty speak in the manner He did in verses 5 to 9 when responding to Aaron and Miriam's rebellious attitude towards Moses. In a prompt show of His indignation and rebuke, He made flippant and disrespectful Miriam leprous! There is a lesson to learn here. Someone might be your friend, your son, your husband, your wife, your daughter, or someone younger than you, but if he or she is under God's anointing and favour to be a leader, you must be careful how you talk about him or her.

When the Lord of all the earth, however, made Miriam leprous, it was the meek Moses who, ironically, pleaded in her behalf, as we can see in verse 13 of the scripture under review. In doing this, Moses, a well-known stammerer, betrayed his countenance to save his elder sister from damnation by pleading for her.

Through the ages, God has not and certainly will not treat lightly anyone who does not hold and stand in awe of His anointed servants. He shares a special covenant and relationship with His anointed servants in distinct ways that no other mortal dared to challenge. Noah found grace in the eyes of the Lord because he 'was a just man, perfect in his generation' and walked with God. God boasted about His servant Job before Satan because he was a 'blameless and upright' man who feared God and shunned evil. His three friends, who did not help matters in his afflictions but imagined that Job's predicament was the result of sin, paid severely when God's wrath was kindled against them, 'For ye have not spoken of Me the thing that is right, as My servant Job hath' (Job 42:7b). It took Job's prayerful intervention to dissuade God from dealing with Eliphaz, Bildad, and Zophar 'after their folly' (verse 8).

In one of Moses's famous encounters with God, the scripture says in Exodus 33:11–23 that he, while praying, wanted to see God's face. The awesome God rather told Moses, 'You can't see my face. If you see my face, you will die. You still have so much work to do for Me. Go behind the rock. I will cover your face with My hand so that when I am passing, I will release My hand so you can see My back.' Glory!

Moses went to where God had directed him. Jehovah passed by but covered the face of His servant Moses, and as God passed, He was proclaiming:

> The LORD, The LORD God gracious and merciful, longsuffering and abounding in steadfastness and

faithfulness, keeping mercy for thousands, forgiving Iniquity and transgression, but by no means clearing the guilty, visiting the iniquity of the fathers upon the children and the children's children to the third and fourth generation. (Exodus 34:6–7)

What does this famous proclamation mean? It means that if your father is a native doctor or a witch doctor, you are already in trouble. Your children and children's children are already in trouble—to the third and fourth generation—unless you *sever* yourself from your father's ancestral lineage by being a believer. Anything short of this puts you under God's wrath, not because of what you have done but because of the outcome of what your parents had done. God repeated what He said in Exodus 20:1–5 by emphatically referring to those who worship other gods as those *who hate him.*

My beloved people, whatever you do now is sure to affect your third and fourth generation. That is what God says. You may not believe it, but you may not be around when God will deal with your children, grandchildren, and great-grandchildren. I always pray for my children. I tell God these words of meditation:

> God, I know You are going to outlive me, but when
> I am no longer here, do not forget my offsprings.
> If You did that for Abraham, do it for me too. The
> blood of Your Son Jesus has atoned for my sins.

My children are going to be really blessed. Someone has already prayed for them in advance. The tremendous privilege and blessing of being born to faithful Christian parents who pray daily for their children is that the Lord will uphold their steps in His path and guide them in their ways.

Queen Jezebel organised a party and asked the people of Jezreel to make Naboth the chairman of the party. In her deception, she gave instructions that they should accuse Naboth of blaspheming against God and the king, and based on that false accusation, they should stone him to death. (Heathen Jezebel had suddenly turned out to be an advocate for Jehovah and was defending him!)

1 Kings 21:1–14 states,

> [1] And it came to pass after these things, that Naboth the Jezreelite had a vineyard, which was in Jezreel, next to the palace of Ahab king of Samaria.
>
> [2] And Ahab spake unto Naboth, saying, Give me thy vineyard, that I may have it for a garden of herbs, because it is near unto my house: and I will give thee for it a better vineyard than it; or, if it seem good to thee, I will give thee the worth of it in money.
>
> [3] And Naboth said to Ahab, The Lord forbid it me, that I should give the inheritance of my fathers unto thee.
>
> [4] And Ahab came into his house heavy and displeased because of the word which Naboth the Jezreelite had spoken to him: for he had said, I will not give thee the inheritance of my fathers. And he laid him down upon his bed, and turned away his face, and would eat no bread.
>
> [5] But Jezebel his wife came to him, and said unto him, Why is thy spirit so sad, that thou eatest no bread?
>
> [6] He said to her, Because I spoke to Naboth, the Jezreelite, and said unto him, Give me thy

7

vineyard for money; or else, if it please thee, I will give thee another vineyard for it: and he answered, I will not give thee my vineyard.

⁷ And Jezebel his wife said unto him, Dost thou now govern the kingdom of Israel? arise, and eat bread, and let thine heart be merry: I will give thee the vineyard of Naboth the Jezreelite.

⁸ So she wrote letters in Ahab's name, and sealed them with his seal, and sent the letters unto the elders and to the nobles that were in his city, dwelling with Naboth.

⁹ And she wrote in the letters, saying, Proclaim a fast, and set Naboth on high among the people:

¹⁰ And set two men, sons of Belial, before him, to bear witness against him, saying, Thou didst blaspheme God and the king. And then carry him out, and stone him, that he may die.

¹¹ And the men of his city, even the elders and the nobles who were the inhabitants in his city, did as Jezebel had sent unto them, and as it was written in the letters which she had sent unto them.

¹² They proclaimed a fast, and set Naboth on high among the people.

¹³ And there came in two men, children of Belial, and sat before him: and the men of Belial witnessed against him, even against Naboth, in the presence of the people, saying, Naboth did blaspheme God and the king. Then they carried

him forth out of the city, and stoned him with stones, that he died.

[14] Then they sent to Jezebel, saying, Naboth is stoned, and is dead.

Jezebel asked her husband to take over Naboth's vineyard after she arranged for his assassination. And then bang! God sent Prophet Elijah to Ahab with proclamations and curses.

1 Kings 21:17–29 states,

> [17] And the word of the Lord came to Elijah the Tishbite, saying,
>
> [18] Arise, go down to meet Ahab king of Israel, which is in Samaria: behold, he is in the vineyard of Naboth, whither he is gone down to possess it.
>
> [19] And thou shalt speak unto him, saying, Thus saith the Lord, Hast thou killed, and also taken possession? And thou shalt speak unto him, saying, Thus saith the Lord, In the place where dogs licked the blood of Naboth shall dogs lick thy blood, even thine.
>
> [20] And Ahab said to Elijah, Hast thou found me, O mine enemy? And he answered, I have found thee: because thou hast sold thyself to work evil in the sight of the Lord.
>
> [21] Behold, I will bring evil upon thee, and will take away thy posterity, and will cut off from Ahab him that pisseth against the wall, and him that is shut up and left in Israel,

²² And will make thine house like the house of Jeroboam the son of Nebat, and like the house of Baasha the son of Ahijah, for the provocation wherewith thou hast provoked me to anger, and made Israel to sin.

²³ And of Jezebel also spake the Lord, saying, The dogs shall eat Jezebel by the wall of Jezreel.

²⁴ Him that dieth of Ahab in the city the dogs shall eat; and him that dieth in the field shall the fowls of the air eat.

²⁵ But there was none like unto Ahab, which did sell himself to work wickedness in the sight of the Lord, whom Jezebel his wife stirred up.

²⁶ And he did very abominably in following idols, according to all things as did the Amorites, whom the Lord cast out before the children of Israel.

²⁷ And it came to pass, when Ahab heard those words, that he rent his clothes, and put sackcloth upon his flesh, and fasted, and lay in sackcloth, and went softly.

²⁸ And the word of the Lord came to Elijah the Tishbite, saying,

²⁹ Seest thou how Ahab humbleth himself before me? because he humbleth himself before me, I will not bring the evil in his days: but in his son's days will I bring the evil upon his house.

Let us see if the proclamation and curse worked.

1 Kings 21:19 states,

> And thou shalt speak unto him, saying, Thus saith the Lord, Hast thou killed, and also taken possession? And thou shalt speak unto him, saying, Thus saith the Lord, In the place where dogs licked the blood of Naboth shall dogs lick thy blood, even thine.

1 Kings 22:33–38 states,

> [33] And it came to pass, when the captains of the chariots perceived that it was not the king of Israel, that they turned back from pursuing him.

> [34] And smote the king of Israel between the joints of the harness: wherefore he said unto the driver of his chariot, Turn thine hand, and carry me out of the host; for I am wounded.

> [35] And the king was stayed up in his chariot against the Syrians, and died at even: and the blood ran out of the wound into the midst of the chariot.

> [36] And there went a proclamation throughout the host about the going down of the sun, saying, Every man to his city, and every man to his own country.

> [37] So the king died, and was brought to Samaria; and they buried the king in Samaria.

> [38] And one washed the chariot in the pool of Samaria; and the dogs licked up his blood; and they washed his armour; according unto the word of the Lord which He spake.

Prophecy no.1 fulfilled.

1 Kings 21:21–22 states,

> [21] Behold, I will bring evil upon thee, and will take away thy posterity, and will cut off from Ahab him that pisseth against the wall, and him that is shut up and left in Israel,

> [22] And will make thine house like the house of Jeroboam the son of Nebat, and like the house of Baasha the son of Ahijah, for the provocation wherewith thou hast provoked me to anger, and made Israel to sin.

2 Kings 10:1–11 states,

> [1] And Ahab had seventy sons in Samaria. And Jehu wrote letters, and sent to Samaria, unto the rulers of Jezreel, to the elders, and to them that brought up Ahab's children, saying,

> [2] Now as soon as this letter cometh to you, seeing your master's sons are with you, and there are with you chariots and horses, a fenced city also, and armour;

> [3] Look even out the best and meetest of your master's sons, and set him on his father's throne, and fight for your master's house.

> [4] But they were exceedingly afraid, and said, Behold, two kings stood not before him: how then shall we stand?

⁵ And he that was over the house, and he that was over the city, the elders also, and the bringers up of the children, sent to Jehu, saying, We are thy servants, and will do all that thou shalt bid us; we will not make any king: do thou that which is good in thine eyes.

⁶ Then he wrote a letter the second time to them, saying, If ye be mine, and if ye will hearken unto my voice, take ye the heads of the men your master's sons, and come to me to Jezreel by tomorrow this time. Now the king's sons, being seventy persons, were with the great men of the city, which brought them up.

⁷ And it came to pass, when the letter came to them, that they took the king's sons, and slew seventy persons, and put their heads in baskets, and sent him them to Jezreel.

⁸ And there came a messenger, and told him, saying, They have brought the heads of the king's sons. And he said, Lay ye them in two heaps at the entering in of the gate until the morning.

⁹ And it came to pass in the morning, that he went out, and stood, and said to all the people, Ye be righteous: behold, I conspired against my master, and slew him: but who slew all these?

¹⁰ Know now that there shall fall unto the earth nothing of the word of the Lord, which the Lord spake concerning the house of Ahab: for the Lord hath done that which he spake by His servant Elijah.

¹¹ So Jehu slew all that remained of the house of Ahab in Jezreel, and all his great men, and his kins folks, and his priests, until he left him none remaining.

Prophecy no. 2 fulfilled.

1 Kings 21:23–24 states,

²³ And of Jezebel also spake the Lord, saying, The dogs shall eat Jezebel by the wall of Jezreel.

²⁴ Him that dieth of Ahab in the city the dogs shall eat; and him that dieth in the field shall the fowls of the air eat.

2 Kings 9:30–37 states,

³⁰ And when Jehu was come to Jezreel, Jezebel heard of it; and she painted her face, and tied her head, and looked out at a window.

³¹ And as Jehu entered in at the gate, she said, Had Zimri peace, who slew his master?

³² And he lifted up his face to the window, and said, Who is on my side? who? And there looked out to him two or three eunuchs.

³³ And he said, Throw her down. So they threw her down: and some of her blood was sprinkled on the wall, and on the horses: and he trode her under foot.

34 And when he was come in, he did eat and drink, and said, Go, see now this cursed woman, and bury her: for she is a king's daughter.

35 And they went to bury her: but they found no more of her than the skull, and the feet, and the palms of her hands.

36 Wherefore they came again, and told him. And he said, This is the word of the Lord, which he spake by his servant Elijah the Tishbite, saying, In the portion of Jezreel shall dogs eat the flesh of Jezebel:

37 And the carcass of Jezebel shall be as dung upon the face of the field in the portion of Jezreel; so that they shall not say, This is Jezebel.

Prophecy no. 3 fulfilled.

King Ahab had thought that one of his seventy children would succeed him as king. But all seventy were killed in one day. Don't you fear God? God must be upheld in awe of His Word, for He is not man as to lie or repent of His utterance. I am talking about the God of Moses, the God of Abraham, the God of Isaac, and the God of Jacob.

God told Abraham in Genesis 12:1–3,

1 Now the Lord had said unto Abram, Get thee out of thy country, and from thy kindred, and from thy father's house, unto a land that I will shew thee:

2 And I will make of thee a great nation, and I will bless thee, and make thy name great; and thou shalt be a blessing:

> ³ And I will bless them that bless thee, and curse him that curseth thee: and in thee shall all families of the earth be blessed.

Genesis 15:13 states,

> And He said unto Abram, Know of a surety that thy seed shall be a stranger in a land that is not theirs, and shall serve them; and they shall afflict them four hundred years.

God told Abraham He would make of Abraham a great nation and that his children and descendants would be in a foreign land for 400 years. By the time of this promise, Abraham's wife was about ninety years, and was not even pregnant. Abraham was about a hundred years. God also promised to bring them out of that land 'with a strong and mighty arm' but that before then . . . 'you shall go to your fathers in peace. You shall be buried at a good old age.'

Abraham died; his son Isaac, the son of promise, died; and Jacob, through Joseph, went to live in Egypt, the foreign land, for about four hundred years. God remembered His promise to Abraham and started working out His own plan and promise to him.

A succinct fulfilmentof this promise is captured in Exodus 12:40:

> Now the sojourning of the children of Israel, who dwelt in Egypt, was four hundred and thirty years.

This number of years may have included the years Joseph lived in Egypt before being joined by his father, Jacob, and his children, as recorded in Acts 7:6:

> And God spake on this wise, That his seed should sojourn in a strange land; and that they should

bring them into bondage, and entreat them evil four hundred years.

God would never forget His promise. That is one incontrovertible thing about God. He will never forget the promises He has made to you.

Numbers 23:19 says,

> God is not a man, that He should lie; neither the son of man, that He should repent: hath He said, and shall He not do it? Or hath He spoken and shall He not make it good?

If God says a thing, it must come to pass. God never fails in His words. I hope that you will spare me the benefit of sharing my personal testimonies here, to avoid not being seen as *blowing my own trumpet*. But whatever I am today, it is just by God's grace.

It does *not puff me up*. If there is anyone marked for being a failure, it is me. If God can do it for me, this same God will also do it for you. God can decide to elevate you and surprise people. He can decide to make those who despise you celebrate you. It is not because you are a prayer warrior or because you are too holy or because of anything so special about you; it is just because of God's grace.

So if your parents have been involved or are involved in the worship of deities, do all you can to be a Christian, a child of God. When you become a believer, you save yourself from God's wrath on the generations and descendants of your parents.

Many years ago, my wife and I prayed:

> Lord, my family, our family—we cut ourselves off from our parents' family and link ourselves and our children and descendants to Jesus Christ.

We do not hate our siblings; on the contrary, we help them as much as we can to walk in the way of the Lord and in several other ways. But my own family remains linked directly to Jesus. All the liabilities and blessings of our parents, we denounced, and we took on ourselves and our descendants all the blessings and liabilities in Jesus Christ our link. We cannot inherit any curse from our parents' families because there is now total severance from their ways and practices that did not honour the Lord God Almighty.

'The LORD, He is God. The LORD, He is God.' The people of Israel, God's own people, God's own firstborn, had been led astray by Ahab's wife, as we have seen here. 'Then you shall say to Pharaoh, Thus says the LORD, Israel is My son, My first born' (Exodus 4:22).

That is what happens when a believer marries an unbeliever; he or she makes the devil his/her father-in-law. In most cases, the child of the devil will lead the child of God astray. This is precisely what happens when a believer is unequally yoked with an unbeliever.

Queen Jezebel was an agent of Satan. She ruled Ahab while Ahab ruled Israel. She made people believe that Baal was the real god.

Elijah the Prophet confronted King Ahab fearlessly and accused him of forsaking the commandments of Jehovah and following Baal.

If you want to provoke God to wrath, go and worship other gods. God did not hide His feelings. He said, 'For I the LORD your God, I'm a jealous God' (Exodus 20:5). God does not accept the worship of other things or gods. True worship exclusively belongs to God,

Jehovah. When you worship other gods or objects, you are simply saying, 'Jehovah, I do not trust you.'

If you are a pastor and you claim you have been called by the Lord Jehovah and you turn round to seek protection or any kind of help from God's enemy, *Satan*, that is an abomination. A simple illustration of such an absurd relationship is when the child of man A goes to seek help from man B, who, incidentally, *is* the enemy of man A. For instance, God called you to preach the gospel, but when you are in trouble or when you want to be seen as succeeding in the ministry, you appeal to Satan to help you.

The devil and Lord God Almighty can never reconcile. Politicians reconcile sooner or later, but there is no way God and Satan will ever reconcile. So when you go to the devil to give you power to do God's work, it is not only an insult to God but a worse case of deception. It will also be an attempt in futility, as such works will be tested by fire. Prophet Elijah challenged King Ahab and all Israel to prove who the true God really is, as we will discover in this scripture:

1 Kings 18:19–24 states,

> [19] Now therefore send, and gather to me all Israel unto mount Carmel, and the prophets of Baal four hundred and fifty, and the prophets of the groves four hundred, which eat at Jezebel's table.

> [20] So Ahab sent unto all the children of Israel, and gathered the prophets together unto mount Carmel.

> [21] And Elijah came unto all the people, and said, How long halt ye between two opinions? if the

Lord be God, follow him: but if Baal, then follow him. And the people answered him not a word.

22 Then said Elijah unto the people, I, even I only, remain a prophet of the Lord; but Baal's prophets are four hundred and fifty men.

23 Let them therefore give us two bullocks; and let them choose one bullock for themselves, and cut it in pieces, and lay it on wood, and put no fire under: and I will dress the other bullock, and lay it on wood, and put no fire under:

24 And call ye on the name of your gods, and I will call on the name of the Lord: and the God that answereth by fire, let him be God. And all the people answered and said, It is well spoken.

Prophet Elijah was so sure that God would not let fire fall from anywhere to consume the sacrifice of the heathen priest.

Elijah told the congregation of Israel that the prophets of Baal, who numbered over four hundred and fifty, should be the first to choose one of the two bulls and pray to their god, Baal, to consume the bull by fire. If Baal did that, then Baal was the true god.

This world belongs to God, and God is in charge of the entire universe. There is nothing to doubt about this. 'The earth is the Lord's and the fullness thereof. The world and those who dwell therein' (Psalm 24:1).

God knows every detail of all events happening everywhere. Nothing takes God unaware. Let us take a little digression from our scriptural reference.

In Brazil, there was a man, a politician called Tancredo Neves. He once said that if only his party, the Social Democratic Party (SDP), could give him 500,000 votes, *not even God* could stop him from being the President of Brazil. All that would make him president was 500,000 votes from his partymen. He got over 500,000 votes during the election. He also won the electoral college. He won the election and was to be sworn in as president of Brazil on 15 March 1985. On 14 March, he was dead, and his vice presidential candidate, José Sarney, was sworn in as president.

You may say it was a coincidence or sheer tragedy, but it was exceptionally *too coincidental*. God is the final voice, the final arbiter who puts people in position.

In Nigeria, there was a man called M. K. O. Abiola who contested and won the election as President of Nigeria in 1994. That election was acclaimed the best, freest, and fairest election Nigeria ever had. Both international and national observers confirmed it. It was a contest between the Social Democratic Party, with Abiola as presidential candidate, and the Nigeria Republican Convention, with Bashir Tofa as presidential candidate.

M. K. O. Abiola had money. M. K. O. Abiola had connections. He was a publisher; the *Concord* newspaper was his own. Concord Airlines was his. The most striking thing about that election was that M. K. O. Abiola, a Muslim, picked Baba Gana Kingibe, another Muslim, as vice presidential candidate. That was the first time and perhaps the last time both the presidential candidate and the running mate in Nigeria were both Muslim. No one expressed concern that both were of one religion. They won more votes in the dominantly Christian south than in the Muslim north. Abiola won the election convincingly, but his own bosom friend, another Muslim, Ibrahim Babangida, the military President of Nigeria at the time, cancelled the election.

All Nigeria, from the east, west, north, and south, unanimously said, 'Yes, Abiola, you will be President of Nigeria.' But God said no. That was the story of that great man *who was conferred with 197 traditional titles by 68 different communities in Nigeria in response to the fact that his financial assistance resulted in the construction of 63 secondary schools, 121 mosques and churches, 41 libraries, 21 water projects in 24 states of Nigeria, and was grand patron to 149 societies and associations in Nigeria.* He won the elections but was never sworn in as the President of Nigeria, probably because *he ordered the sinking of three million copies of the Bible in the high sea. The container load of the holy book was bound for Nigeria when he used his influence to cease and destroy them. The Christian world did not bat an eyelid. I think God was apparently paying him and his family back.*

The unfortunate incident was captured in an account credited to one Mohammed Haruna, who wrote in a newspaper column:

> "The Bishop of Akure, The Rt. Rev. Emmanuel B. Gbonigi, at the wake of the annulment of the Presidential elections of 1993, alluded to the fact that it was Abiola who went and sank a ship that was bringing bibles and Christian hymn books to Nigeria. We demonstrated in Akure against Abiola in those days."

It is strange that a man who was said to have sponsored the building of mosques and churches went to the extent of destroying bibles, if that story is to be taken seriously. However, no one has ever deliberately insulted God and got away with it.

John Lennon, one of the Beatles (a musical group), said in 1966:

> Christianity will go. It will vanish and shrink. I needn't argue about that. I'm right and will be

proved right. We are more popular than Jesus now. I don't know which will go first—rock 'n' roll and Christianity.

Fourteen years later, Lennon was shot dead by Mark David Chapman in New York City on 8 December 1980.

Brazilian singer Cazuza died at the age of thirty-two after blowing cigarette smoke at God during a show in Rio de Janeiro. While smoking his cigarette, he puffed out some smoke into the air and said, 'God, that's for you.'

Marilyn Monroe, an actress, told Billy Graham that she did not need Jesus, and she died shortly afterwards.

In Campinas, Brazil, a group of friends were drunk and went to pick up a friend. The mother accompanied her daughter to the car and was so worried about the drunkenness of her friends, and holding her hand, she said to her daughter, who was already seated in the car, 'My daughter, go with God, and may He protect you.' The daughter replied, 'Only if He [God] travels in the trunk, because inside here, it's already full.'

Hours later, news came to the mother that the group had a fatal accident in which everyone died. The car was damaged beyond recognition, but surprisingly, the trunk was intact. The police said there was no way the trunk could have remained intact. To their surprise, inside the trunk was a crate of eggs, and none were broken. *Jesus was in the trunk!*

Christine Hewitt, a Jamaican journalist and entertainer, said the Bible (the Word of God) was the worst book ever written. In June 2006, she was found burnt beyond recognition in her motor vehicle.

In this country, those of you who are old enough know Abiola. Abiola's election was the best election Nigeria ever had. The voting process was organised using the clumsy Option A4, in which voters lined up behind the candidate they preferred. Nigeria would never have that kind of election again and had not had it before. It was the freest and fairest election that Nigeria could ever have. It was between the SDP and NRC. The SDP won. Abiola had connections, and I don't think there is any man who could have had such overwhelming connections in Nigeria than Abiola. He had the money. When he flew out of the country, Abiola did not go with any serious luggage, because he had a house in almost every city in the world. He had the Concord Press, publishers of the *Concord* newspapers, airplanes—everything. He had connections and won the election, gathering more votes in the dominantly Christian south than the Muslim north. Don't forget the fact that Abiola was a Muslim, and Kingibe, his running mate, was a Muslim also; it had never happened before. And they won the election—two Muslims. Ordinarily, Nigerians, especially the Christian south enclave, would not have accepted a Muslim–Muslim ticket, but they accepted and voted for both men in spite of their religious persuasion. Abiola was not a wicked man, but going out of the way to buy all the bibles and destroy them was one singular act too many to provoke God to wrath. He couldn't become the president of this country. No one can insult God and get away with it—nobody.

So Elijah told Ahab, 'Call your prophets. We shall give them one bull. They should pray to their god. They are over four hundred and fifty. Then the God that answers by fire . . .'

Lyric: The God that answereth by fire, He shall be my God. (2×)

Ahab was confident that the prophets of Baal would win. If he didn't believe it, he wouldn't have accepted the contest. He would perhaps have told Elijah to discard the proposal entirely. But he accepted it. He gathered all Israel for the contest at Mount Carmel. They prayed, and they played. It didn't work, from morning, according to the Bible, until noon. Elijah mockingly said, 'Please cry aloud, for he is god. Either he is meditating or he is busy or he is on a journey or perhaps he is sleeping and must be awakened.' But the Bible says, 'The Lord our God neither slumbers nor sleeps.' If God sleeps for one second, the devil will finish us. If God sleeps for one second alone, hey! *palava*. Our God never takes a vacation. He never sleeps. He never slumbers. He never gets weary. He never gets tired. At times, I say, 'How does God do all this?' When there is daylight in the USA and it is midnight in Australia at the same time, He is in charge, and people are praying to Him round the clock. When it is nightfall in Nigeria, it is morning somewhere else. That is why people are seen to be praying round the clock, and He monitors what is happening everywhere at the same time.

> Chorus: You are the mighty man in battle, El Shaddai. You are the mighty man in battle, Jehovah-Nissi. You are the mighty man in battle, El Shaddai. You are the mighty man in battle. Glory to Your name.

So they got their sacrifice and prayed and prayed until they were tired. Elijah relieved them in their hopelessness when he stopped them, realising that they would have continued endlessly praying to a lifeless god.

Many years ago, I was in my house, eating with my wife. One elderly woman came in and said, 'Thank God I have found You. My daughter will rise up again.' I said, 'Mama, what is happening now?' She said, 'My daughter is dead.' I felt my heart pounding in my chest. She said that since she had found me, her daughter would get well. I got up and followed her but pondered why this woman had turned to a huge temptation by her near-impossible request. Her daughter was dead, and she had come to me to raise her from the dead. When we got there, the lady was really lying dead. People had gathered and were crying in the house. My heart started pumping more blood out of fear. I thought in my heart that if this thing did not work, they would say that I was not a man of God. But I also had the option to ask my wife to come and call me ten minutes later so I could have an excuse to leave. However, I didn't tell her. So when we got there, the woman was so confident.

The woman attended another church. I am an Anglican pastor, so I was surprised that she came to ask me, an Anglican pastor, to come and pray.

When I got there, I prayed and prayed in English, to the point that I started "speaking in tongues". I didn't have any hope, to some extent. The woman told me to pray that her daughter would wake up. I thought to myself, *This woman doesn't know what she is talking about.* The dead lady was married, with two children. I prayed relentlessly for more than thirty minutes. Nothing happened.

I said to myself, 'My God, if I had known, I would have told my wife ahead of time to subsequently call me up and say that I am needed urgently.' However, after sustained prayer, the God of heaven and earth responded, and suddenly, the lady sneezed. With the hope of restoring the lady back to life clearly evident, I raised the tempo of my prayer power, and to the glory of God, she got up. I must admit here that as a mortal being, I did nothing outside the power of the Holy Ghost. In fact, the miraculous intervention from God was out of the sheer faith of the woman. Otherwise, I didn't believe the woman would rise again. The shivery hands of a sighing, weeping dying generation of people are outstretched, and their hearts are open, seeking help. Those people will believe and receive Jesus when they see the same power and miracles that He performed on earth being performed in lives today.

So Elijah saved these people because they were praying persistently. When he called on the people, 'Come near to me,' all the people quickly drew nearer to him. And with the assurance that he would repair the altars that were broken, the stage was set for the glorious contest. He took twelve stones, according to the number of the tribes of sons of Jacob, to whom the Lord God had said, 'Israel shall be your name.' Then he arranged the stones and put the bullock on top of it. But do you know one amazing thing Elijah did? He said they should pour water. If I were him, I wouldn't prefer the pouring of water but rather something that would make the fire burn quickly. He first chose the pouring of water when they wanted fire for the burnt sacrifice. Verse 33 of that scripture says, 'And he put the wood in order, cut the bull in pieces and laid it on the wood and said, "fill four water-pots with water, and pour it on the burnt sacrifice and on the wood."' In verse 34, he called on them to pour the water a second time and a third time, because he was so sure that his God would do it. Little wonder, he personally filled the trench with water (verse 35b).

Many of us would want to help God. Don't help God. Do not help God do His work. Don't help God. Uzziah wanted to help God, and God struck him dead. Don't help God. Some people are quick to say, 'Heaven helps those who help themselves.' I challenge those who claim and adhere to this interpretation of the Bible, to show us any single passage in the Bible that even alludes to such a thought. Most surprisingly, some adherents to the Christian faith often take the scriptures out of context to justify actions or ways of life that do not honour God. 'Give to Caesar what belongs to Caesar and give to God what belongs to God', for instance, is in the Bible, but it doesn't mean that while you worship God in church, you should also pay homage to a juju priest in his shrine or join in celebrating a pagan festival. It doesn't mean that at all. If you place your trust in this God, I am confident—I am sure of what I'm saying, have proved Him and tried him—that it is going to work. God will protect you.

Exuding absolute confidence in the King of the universe, the One who has all power in heaven and earth, Elijah set the stage, ready to announce who the true God is by praying to Him who also readily answers prayers. Just hear his prayer: 'Lord God of Abraham, Isaac, and Israel, let it be known this day that You are the God in Israel and I am Your servant and I have done all these at Your word. Hear me, oh Lord, hear me that these people may know that You are the Lord God and that You have turned Your heart back to them again.' Then fire came and consumed the sacrifice. The Bible says the fire consumed everything. Hear what it says: 'The fire of the Lord fell and consumed the sacrifice and the wood and the water and the dust, and it licked up the water that was in the trench.' And what did the people say? They fell down and said, 'The Lord Jehovah, He is God. The Lord He is God.' They were convinced beyond all doubts that Jehovah is Lord, is God, was God, and will remain God forever; He will never change.

This God has not changed. He is still the same God. If you are in the church, hear the pertinent question Elijah put before the people, including the perplexed King Ahab: 'How long will you be limping between two opinions?' How long? And I ask: how long? Many of us are in cults, some of us are in secret societies, and some of us go to native doctors for help.

They may have their own power, but their power is limited. 'Man pass man, juju pass juju, but God pass all.' God is the ultimate. He is all in all. Anything that God cannot do for you, no one else can do for you. He is the supreme. Igbos call Him *Chineke nke puru ime ihenile* because they don't know how to describe Him.

They call Him 'God who can do everything'. Our God is supreme. All throughout the entire scripture, He never failed anyone. He can never fail you; He never fails anybody. If God says a thing, it must surely come to pass. God never loses any battle; He never loses any war. There are times it may look as if He is losing, but

He triumphs in the end. Why do we go to lesser gods and leave the main God? Why do we leave God, who is the supreme and the sovereign Lord?

I was preaching somewhere in the year 2000. Women were sitting on one side and men on the other side. As I climbed the pulpit, the women were precisely sitting at my right-hand side. One woman suddenly fell down. I saw her. The ushers came and carried her out to the vestry. I continued preaching. After preaching, I came down. Two persons came to call me from the vestry. They asked me, 'Did you see one woman fall down when you were preaching?' I replied, 'Yes, I saw her.' A lady said that they had seen fire from the pulpit, so they had thought it was anointing from me. The woman in question confessed that some people had given her charms to kill me, and the fire had consumed the charms in her hand. After the service that day (it was a Sunday), between 6 and 7 p.m., a man and his wife came to my house; we were staying in the cathedral then. I was upstairs when my children called my attention to a man and a woman who had come to see me. I was not moved to see them or know who they were, because I felt it was too late to receive any visitors at that time.

Two days later, they came again at that same time. I said to myself, 'Why are these people coming by at this time?' They should have come in the morning or in the afternoon. I didn't know it was this same woman who had been coming with her husband. After two weeks, reports came that the woman had died. I did not know her, of course. I never had any interaction with her.. It is possible I may not know you, and you may not know me intimately, other than on the basis of a pastor–member relationship. In my whole life experience in the ministry, what has often bothered me and troubled my heart is situations where some people (Christians) have made spirited efforts to kill me. I ponder on why such people harbour such wicked thoughts in their hearts.

If I prefer a pastor to canon and someone would want to kill him, why not kill me, who made him canon? But hear the Word of the Lord as written in 1 John 5:18b: 'He who has been born of God keeps himself and the wicked one does not touch him.'

And the scriptures say, '[Kattey] Your life is hidden with Christ in God' (Colossians 3:3, word in brackets is mine). So if you want to kill me now, God bless you. You will kill God the Father first; then God the Son; God the Holy Spirit; the archangels Michael, Gabriel, Uriel, and Raphael; the four living creatures; and the twenty-four elders. You will also kill the cherubim and seraphim, all the angelic hosts in heaven. Then you can have access to kill me. Is it possible? To do so is *mission impossible*; this is because I have the gene of the Father, the awesome God, who is all-powerful. *No shaking, nothing mega!*

If you are a Christian, your life is hidden with Christ inside God. It is not fiction; it is not dogma. It is an eternal truth. The scripture in Ephesians 2:6–7 clearly defines our citizenship in heaven as coheirs with Jesus. It says, 'I sit together in heavenly places in Christ Jesus.' Again, in Luke 10:19, Jesus said, 'I have given you authority to thread upon serpents and scorpions and upon all the powers of the enemy, and nothing shall by any means hurt you.' When all the powers of the enemy are under your foot, it also means you have dominion over witchcraft spells, sorcery, native doctors and their incantations, enchantment, and divination because you sit in heavenly places in Christ Jesus; the snares of fowlers do not have sway over you. Another assurance given to us as believers is eloquently expressed in Isaiah 54:17: 'No weapon [fashioned, formed, contrived, formulated, or designed] against you shall prosper.'

It is in the Bible, and I believe the Bible. Let me tell you one good thing the Lord has done for me that makes me believe him. It is not by my power; God has made me believe him. Anything He has said, I believe.

Chorus: God said it. I believe it. That settles it. (2×)

When we are talking about the awesome power of God in the life of a believer, we are not referring to something ephemeral or temporary, but to life and evident testimonies of the limitless power of God. Let me share another heart-warming encounter and victory that the Lord gave us. My daughter married in December 2010 and became pregnant later. She was in the hospital. She said that at night, a hand stretched through the window of the three-storey building where she was accommodated. Do you understand what I am saying? Every night, a hand would stretch towards her through the window of the third floor of a building where she was hospitalised, not the ground floor. My wife and I told her to come back home and stay with us. She came that night, and in the course of the still night, at about 2 a.m., she got up and called Mummy and said, 'Somebody opened the door.' But the door was locked. You know, witches can enter a room well locked; if you are a witch, you will understand what I am saying.

I will tell you why I say so. My daughter said that somebody opened the door (the door was locked) and entered her body and made her start wriggling. I said, 'Let us go down and see. It is an insult to me in my own compound.' I didn't wear any episcopal vestments (for it is not the hood that makes the monk); I didn't wear anything but our normal sleeping dress. It was 2 a.m. We opened my door and went down. When we got to her room, I said, 'I am the Archbishop of this area.' I remember saying, 'Cross River, Akwa Ibom, Rivers, and Bayelsa, all their powers are under my control. All the witches and wizards are under my control. All the powers, Ogboni people, are under my control. You can't come and insult me.' Then I commanded them to leave my daughter. 'Pack your load and leave my daughter.' My daughter said, 'Daddy, they are going.' Why wouldn't they go? I have been given the authority over the whole Ecclesiastical Province of Niger Delta and the Church of Nigeria to trample on serpents and scorpions and over all the powers of the enemy now that I am the Dean by virtue of my position as most senior archbishop. Now that I am the Dean, the whole country is my territory.

If, for instance, you are a recognised chief of a village and you think that your subjects will kill you, you are a *foolish* chief. My father was a chief, a government-recognised chief. I became a born-again Christian in 1971. One day, somebody came to him and said, 'Sir, Chief, somebody invoked juju against me.' He gave some money to my father, as the custom demanded; I don't know how much he gave. My father sat in his chair; he used to read the Bible, and he used to sing hymns too. After about thirty minutes, the man came back and said, 'Chief, I am afraid, oh, I am afraid. Please call the man and beg him so that he can revoke the juju.' My father said, 'All the juju in this place are under my control now. I am the chief. They cannot operate without my permission.'

That day, it dawned on me that as a Christian, a child of God, I have more power than my father. Yes! You are the chief of a place, and someone thinks juju can kill you. Listen, when you take to the throne as chief of a place, it means everybody has relinquished their powers to you. That is what it means. If you are the chief of a community, all powers have been surrendered to you; all the powers are under your control. So what I am saying is not theory; it is practical.

God is real; God is not a phenomenon that happened by chance. You know, God controls this universe, and whatever He says in His Word must surely come to pass. The people who gathered at the contest at Mount Carmel confessed, 'The Lord, He is God. Jehovah, He is God.' I don't know how many people are still getting power from native doctors and witch doctors. No matter how efficient and powerful they are, if you mention my name to them, they may have never seen me before, but they will warn you never to mention my name again in their shrine or within their hearing. They will tell you, 'That man is not a good man.' I will never be a good man to the devil and his agents. Why? My name is hidden with Christ in God. And again, 'The Name of the LORD is a strong tower; the righteous hides in that Name and is safe' (Proverbs 18:10). My name is hidden in the name of Jesus. I am righteous because of Jesus Christ. God looks at me, and God sees me through Christ Jesus. A pair of glasses makes people with poor sight see more clearly. When Yahweh, the God of Israel, sees me through His Son Jesus Christ, all my sins contract to zero, so I become righteous. But if God were to see me outside of Christ, not only my good deeds but also my very self becomes a filthy rag. 'For we are all as unclean thing. And all our righteousness are like filthy rags' (Isaiah 64:6). That is what being without Jesus Christ feels like.

In the early 1970s, there was a boy, a devout Christian, who every morning would devote himself to singing praises in loud christian lyrics that often disturbed the peace of the compound, which accommodated other tenants of a particular set of beliefs or the other, or of every shade of religious persuasion. The compound, which was square-shaped, had a common kitchen and a bathroom accessible to every tenant.

One fateful Monday morning, a man who was one of the occupants of the compound planted poison in the boy's pot of soup, which was on the fire, while the boy was in the bathroom. The evil man was able to do that because it was a common kitchen, and he was driven to the wicked act possibly because he could no longer accommodate the noisy boy and his loud lyrics that often stole the man's peace, disturbing the entire neighbourhood. The man felt that the best thing he could do in the circumstance was do away with the boy through food poisoning. To his surprise, the boy had a meal of *eba* (cassava flour) and the soup to his satisfaction and hurried to his place of work. The evil man, in frustration, lashed out at the boy and, seizing him by his neck, began to shout insults at him, saying, 'You are a bad boy! You just use the church as a cover!' He repeatedly called the shell-shocked boy a bad boy before an undiscerning crowd of people who had now gathered at the scene of the unfolding drama. The evil man confessed that over the weekend, he travelled home and returned with some fetish poison which he poured into the christian man's soup in the kitchen when the christian man was having his showers. And that the boy ate the poisoned food without harm and was going to work. He was calling the innocent boy a bad boy. The curious and confused crowd could not pass any judgement or join issues with either of the two. Who then is the bad person—the man, or the boy whom the man could not kill?

The Lord, He is God. The Lord, He is God. Let us pray.

Prayer: Lord, You are God. Lord, You are God. You are God of heaven and earth. All things are in Your hands to do or not to do. You are sovereign. You have the final say in all matters. We pray, show Your unlimited power in our midst. Smash and dismantle every conspiracy against us, and give us victory over forces that work against us. In Jesus's name, we pray. Amen.

2

DAY 2

Theme: 'The Lord, He is God. The Lord, He is God.'

In our talk on Day 1 of our exhortation, we acknowledged that the Lord is Jehovah. He is the LORD, not the Lord. In continuation of our theme, I am reading from Daniel 3:28–29:

> Nebuchadnezzar spake and said, blessed be the God of Shadrach, Meshach and Abednego who hath sent His angel and delivered His servants that trusted in Him, and yielded their bodies, that they might not serve nor worship any god except their own God. Therefore I make a decree that every people, nation, or language which speak anything amiss against the God of Shadrach, Meshach and Abednego shall be cut in pieces, and their houses shall be made a dunghill because there is no other God that can deliver like this sort.

This was a heathen king; he neither knew God nor contemplated serving him. He had his own gods. He did not have any idea of the

Jehovah God we worship today, but he intuitively acknowledged Him as the Lord God Almighty when he said, 'Blessed be the God of Shadrach, Meshach, and Abednego.' The subject matter, for emphasis and reference, is not Shadrach, Meshach, and Abednego but the *God of* Shadrach, Meshach, and Abednego. It is all about God! That a heathen king would submit to our awesome God and praise Him and that we who call ourselves Christians would go and worship other gods is appalling and most shameful. There are people here who worship other gods and, at the same time, claim to serve or worship Jehovah God. They are, to say the least, hypocrites.

Nobody sees you, but God sees you. Nobody knows what you do, but God knows what you do. There is somebody here just last two weeks. You went to consult a juju (witch doctor). It is not going to help you. (This is "word of knowledge.)

Nebuchadnezzar was a king who exercised tremendous authority over a very vast area of land up to Ethiopia. (In those days, it was the ancient kingdom of Babylon, which we call Iran today. Persia was around that area.) He ruled over the whole place. There is every need for us, as a church, to pray for our kings, leaders, Bishops, archdeacons, and pastors, because they can wake up one morning and do anything and say anything that may not augur well with us. It behoves us to pray for our governors and the president. The president can wake up tomorrow morning and declare a two-day public holiday without giving any reason. You must obey him.

If you pray for them, they will not make mistakes easily. But if you go on criticising them always, they may make mistakes. Don't forget that we are bound by the command in the Word of God to pray for those in authority, and if we don't, we must accept responsibility for their mistakes and failures. If the Bible says we should pray for our leaders whether we like them or not, then we must pray for them. The Bible did not say that if we like them, we pray for them. No. We must pray for all those in leadership because they may think evil things and do them.

The Bible says Nebuchadnezzar woke up one morning and asked people to build an image of gold that was ninety feet tall and nine feet wide. The image of gold referred to here was almost taller than an eight-storey building. It was completely made of gold. But whether it is made of silver or gold or wood, an image is an image.

The scripture admonishes in Exodus 20:5, 'Thou shall not bow down to any carved image whether of gold or silver or anything.' Some people today worship the sun and stars, while others worship snakes. There are even those who keep snakes in their bedrooms and worship them as gods. How can somebody have snakes in his bedroom? Some people in the occult forbid women from stepping into a particular room in their residence because they believe and are given instructions that women would desecrate their charms and shrines in the room, and these people are in the church! And perhaps they are leaders in the church!

Some years ago, there was a man who was in a cult and who used to disappear to attend meetings. When he entered his bedroom, he would go out of his body for an astral journey, but the rule was that the door must be securely locked. So one fateful night, this man went and slept on the bed without locking his door. He travelled out of his body. He would go and do all sorts of things outside, and his wife didn't know. His wife knocked on the door and opened it, calling him, 'Darling, darling.' The man was sleeping, but he was off; he was not there. She touched the man and shook his body in an attempt to wake him from 'sleep', but to no avail. The secret of their art is that if you move their body from the position it is in before the journey, they can't come back to their body again. That is why they lock their doors.

When the man came back, the body had moved a little, so he couldn't enter it again. He tried to enter, but he couldn't enter his body. Our God can make you make a mistake if you are in the occult and in the habit of attacking His people. I always tell God to cause those who would want to attack me or my family to fail their own rules. The reason is that when they fail their rules whatever they are doing backfires on them.

You see a delicate thing; it is a very delicate thing. People take big risks worshiping the devil. However, this man prayed that if God would allow him to enter his body again, he would be a Christian. He said, 'Jesus, help me enter this body.' He tried again, and he entered his body. The man abandoned everything and became a Christian.

I am a Christian. If you like carry hundreds of flames behind me, it will not hurt me. For some people, carrying flames of fire behind them invalidates their charms. But if you pass live fire behind me several times, I will never be moved, because my Jesus is also a consuming fire. Some people don't look at dead bodies even, because if they do, their charms will become powerless. So they will not look at a dead body, even if their own loved one dies; they simply keep away.

Do you know that some people who we think are mad are not mad after all? Some people are told to be mad for ten years or so, and when they recover, they are promised a lot of money. So all these people who are seen to be mad, all of them are not really mad. Some people will go and feign madness. They eat all the rubbish. After ten years or seven years, as the case may be, they will go back and become very wealthy.

There was this man from Arbmana (name of place disguised deliberately) who came back from Lagos and gave a blanket to his father. It was during harmattan period, so he wanted his father to cover himself with the blanket. At night, he would go see his father to check if he had used it. The father would not cover himself. The man said to his father, 'Papa, don't you use the blanket?' The father said, 'I will use it.' Every night, the man would go and ask his father to use the blanket. One day, the young man was having his siesta. The father went and covered him with the blanket, and the man became naira under it. He had wanted to use his father to make money. So the father told people what happened. They carried the money and buried it. Why would you want to use your father to make money? Why? A human being that God made, you want to use him for a moneymaking ritual?

Nebuchadnezzar set up this gigantic image, ninety feet tall, nine feet wide, and commanded that all officers of the government must bow down to the image; in fact, he ordered not only the officers but everybody. He set a day for the dedication and called the satraps, the judges, the commissioners, and the ministers, and they gathered round for the dedication of this image. He said, 'When you hear the flute, the cymbals, and the trumpet, you bow down and worship this image.' They were doing this in his presence. They gathered that day for the inauguration of that image; they blew the trumpet, the flute, the harp, and the lyre. They played the guitars. There was noise everywhere, and everybody bowed down to the image.

But there were three men—Shadrach, Meshach, and Abednego—who were original Jews. They were not the only Jews there; other Jews bowed down. Other Jews bowed down, so they didn't have any problem. But these three men said, 'No, we have been told not to worship any other god than Jehovah God. Jehovah God is the only God we ought to worship, and no other god.' The Jews would never worship any other god, no matter the circumstance, and other officers reported the three stubborn slaves to the king. They said, 'King, you made a law, but there are three Jews who you put in high position who have made nonsense of your law and refused to bow down to the big image you made with gold. They refused to bow down, and they are Jews.' The three Jews had a disadvantage because they were slaves from a foreign country, but luckily, they had been made officers. It was a big credit to them but also a disadvantage, and they didn't care about losing their jobs for the sake of this God. They said they were going to serve God, and God only: 'Take your position from us if you like.' The king invited them and said, 'Of all the people in my kingdom, are you the only Jews? Bow down to my image and go and serve your Jehovah. I was told that the three of you do not want to serve this image.' They responded, 'Yes, our king'. He said, 'Maybe there is a mistake. I will tell the musicians to play the instruments now. You bow down and go back to your positions.' The three men said no.

The king said, 'If you are ready as you hear the sound of the horn, flute, harp, lyre, and symphony with other instruments and you fall down and worship the image I have made, well and good. But if you do not worship, you will be cast immediately into the midst of the fiery furnace. If you refuse to worship this image, I will cast you into the fire.' But he made a mistake. If he had ended it at that, it perhaps would have been good for him. Hear what he added: 'And let me see the God who will deliver you from my hands.' Apparently, in saying that, the king crossed the red line. He brought God into the matter. When somebody tells you that if you pray, he will so deal with you no matter the God you serve, go and sleep. He has brought God into the matter. He has challenged God.

When somebody comes to attack a child of God, he/she is not the focus of the attack but God. The king said, 'And let me see the God . . .' That was where Shadrach, Meshach, and Abednego won the battle. When someone comes and threatens you and says 'I will so deal with you that God will forget you', go and sleep. God will fight for you. I say God will fight for you. The king made a mistake by *dragging* God into the matter. You don't joke with God that way.

See, our God is a personality. He is not just air and is not just wind. He is a personality who controls the whole universe. He knows I am here now; He knows you are right here now. He knows your name; God can call you by name. He says He knows the number of hairs on your head. God is not a joker.

Samuel was asked to go and anoint a king from Jesse's family, and when he got there, the children lined up. David must have asked, 'Daddy, what is happening today? It seems you are preparing to host an important visitor'. His father may have replied, 'Sonny (that is, my son), it is not for you. It is for your big brothers. Go to the farm and take care of our sheep. It is not for you.' David may have said, 'Daddy, let me stay and watch.' The father probably insisted that David should go, as it was not for him: 'Go to the bush. Don't worry us here. We don't want any disturbance. This is serious business and not for small boys.'

Samuel wanted to anoint Eliab at first; God said no, for God sees not as man sees. God looks into the heart; men look on the outside.

Another person came, and God said, 'Don't anoint.' Samuel went through seven of them, and God said, 'Don't anoint.' When Samuel asked Jesse if there was anybody he had not seen, 'Yes, there is one small boy. I asked him to go and look after our sheep. He is not fit for this type of work. Choose any of these ones here. The boy is a small boy.' But Samuel said, 'Go and call him. Let's see him.' As the boy was coming, God said to Samuel, 'Anoint him.' That's the way God operates. You don't need to be there; you don't need to be there at all. Why do you bother to be there? Anywhere you are, God will identify you. God will locate you.

See, there is nothing like *luck* in the world, or coincidence; everything is ordered by God. If you are here tonight, it is not luck, and it is not coincidence; God wants you to be here tonight.

And so Shadrach, Meshach, and Abednego said,

> O! Nebuchadnezzar, we have no need to answer you in this matter, but if that is the case, our God whom we serve is able to deliver us from your hands, but even if He does not deliver us we shall still not serve your god.

Our God is sovereign. He does whatever pleases Him, at His discretion. If you think about God, you wonder who this God is. What God will do for you might not be what He will do for me. Look at Aaron, an ordained priest. Aaron made a golden calf, and Israel, a chosen generation of God's people, started worshiping the golden calf. God didn't punish Aaron. But when God said to Moses, 'Speak to the rock,' and Moses hit the rock instead, God punished him by preventing him from entering the Promised Land. The way God treats me may not be the way He will treat you. The manner and way I may do a thing and get away with it may not be the same manner and way you do the same thing and get away with it. You can't judge God that way.

Look at Solomon, the son of a distrustful woman named Bathsheba. Of all the children of David, God chose him to be the king of Israel. Have you heard of a thing like that before? If it were by secular election, Solomon would have failed the election. The electorate would have dismissed him, saying, 'Like Mama, like son.' God, however, chose this young man and made him king of Israel.

John the Baptist was in prison for a little while when he proclaimed himself the forerunner of Christ. They killed him in prison, but Peter was delivered by God out of prison. So God decides anything under heaven at His discretion and as it pleases Him. That is what makes Him thesoverign Lord!

The three Hebrew men said, 'If God does not deliver us from your hand, we will die, but we believe He is going to do it.' And the king became angry at the strangers—slaves at that—for the attitude of the three friends was an affront to his office as king. You can insult a man in authority privately and get away with it, but not publicly. If you see somebody in his office and tell him, 'Master, I will deal with you. I will kick you. I will slap you,' he can overlook your threats. But if you do so publicly, the man will sack you or deal with you in a manner that could be better imagined. People were there, and they were seeing Shadrach, Meshach, and Abednego defying the king, King Nebuchadnezzar. The king got angry and said, 'Go and heat the furnace seven times more to teach them a lesson, and I will see the God that will come and deliver them.' His soldiers went and made the furnace seven times hotter, as he ordered.

So Nebuchadnezzar commanded his soldiers to throw the three friends into the burning furnace. The scripture here says, 'Then Nebuchadnezzar was full of fury and the expression on his face showed towards Shadrach, Meshach, and Abednego. He spoke and commanded that the heat in the furnace be increased seven times more than it was usually heated, and he commanded certain mighty men of valour who were in his army to bind Shadrach, Meshach, and Abednego and cast them into the fiery furnace. Then these men were bound in their coats, their trousers, their turbans, and other garments, and they were cast into the depths of the fiery furnace.' The king himself supervised his own order, to ensure there were no lapses.

Therefore, hear this: 'Because the king's command was urgent [harsh] and the furnace was exceedingly hot, the heat from the fire killed those men who took Shadrach, Meshach, and Abednego into the furnace.' The soldiers who took them there were all killed by the heat. But something happened; the king, while still angry and watching, saw four men. He called the people around him in bewilderment to find out how many men were thrown into the fire. They told him there were three: Shadrach, Meshach, and Abednego. The king said, 'But I see a fourth man that looks like a son of a god. He is not human, and He is not from this realm. He is not human. His clothes are glittering and shining.' But who is this man, this special man that the king saw? He is the King of kings and the Lord of lords, the Alpha and Omega, the Beginning and the End, the First and the Last, the Lion of the Tribe of Judah, the Rock of Ages, the Good Shepherd, the Commander-in-Chief of His own army of angels, the Master of all grand masters.

Interlude of song:

> Je-sus, Je-sus (2×)
> Your name is a miracle
> Your name is a comforter
> Your name is a mighty God, Je-sus

Nebuchadnezzar, the king, said, 'I see the fourth man there.' That fourth man is always with you anywhere you are. There were three men in the fire, but that fourth man possibly may not have been seen by Shadrach, Meshach, and Abednego. The Bible says even the chain used in tying them was melted. They were walking in the fire. Nothing happened to their hair. The part of their body that should have been burnt first was intact—the hair. They were walking in the fire, singing this popular canticle (according to Jewish legends):

Benedicite Omnia Opera

[1] O All ye works of the *Lord* / bless ye the / Lord:

Praise Him and / magnify / Him for / ever.

[2] O ye Angels of the *Lord* / bless ye The / Lord: *Praise* Him and / magni-fy Him for / ever.

[3] O ye *Heavens* / bless ye the / Lord: *Praise* Him and / magni-fy / Him for / ever.

[4] O ye waters that be above the *Firmament* / bless ye the / Lord: *Praise* Him and / magn-ify / Him for / ever.

[5] O all ye powers of the *Lord* / bless ye the / Lord: *Praise* Him and / magni-fy / Him for / ever.

[6] O ye sun and *moon* / bless ye the / Lord: *Praise* Him and / magni-fy / Him for / ever.

[7] O ye stars of *Heaven* / bless ye the / Lord: *Praise* Him and / magni-fy / Him for / ever.

[8] O ye showers and *Dews* / bless ye the / Lord: *Praise* Him and / magni-fy / Him for / ever.

[9] O ye winds of *God* / bless ye the / Lord: *Praise* Him and / magni-fy/ Him for / ever.

[10] O ye fire and *heat* / bless ye the / Lord: *Praise* **Him** and / magni-fy / Him for / ever.

[11] O ye winter and *summer* / bless ye the / Lord: *Praise* Him and / magni-fy / Him for / ever.

[12] O ye dews and *frost* / bless ye the / Lord: *Praise* Him and / magni-fy / Him for / ever.

[13] O ye frost and *cold* / bless ye the / Lord: *Praise* Him and / magni-fy / Him for / ever.

[14] O ye ice and *snow* / bless ye the / Lord: *Praise* **Him** and / magni-fy / Him for / ever.

¹⁵ O ye nights and *day* / bless ye the / Lord: *Praise* Him and / magni-fy / Him for / ever.

¹⁶ O ye light and *darkness* / bless ye the / Lord: *Praise* Him and / magni-fy / Him for / ever.

¹⁷ O ye lightens and *clouds* / bless ye the / Lord: *Praise* **Him** and / magni-fy / Him for / ever.

¹⁸ O let the *earth* / bless the / Lord: yea, let it *Praise* Him and / magni-fy / Him for / ever.

¹⁹ O ye mountains and *hills* / bless ye the / Lord: *Praise* Him and / magni-fy / Him for / ever.

²⁰ O all ye green things upon the *Earth* / bless ye the / Lord: *Praise* Him and / magni-fy / Him for / ever.

²¹ O ye *wells* / bless ye the Lord: *Praise* Him and / magni-fy / Him for / ever.

²² O ye seas and *floods* / bless ye the / Lord: *Praise* Him and / magni-fy / Him for / ever.

²³ O ye whales and all that move in the *waters* / bless ye the / Lord: *Praise* / Him and / magni-fy Him for / ever.

²⁴ O all ye fowls of the *air* / bless ye the / Lord: *Praise* Him and / magni-fy / Him for / ever.

²⁵ O all ye beasts and *cattle* / bless ye the / Lord: *Praise* Him and / magni-fy / Him for / ever.

²⁶ O ye children of *men* / bless ye the / Lord: *Praise* Him and / magni-fy / Him for / ever.

[27] O let *Israel* / bless the / Lord: *Praise* Him and / magni-fy / Him for / ever.

[28] O ye priests of the *Lord* / bless ye the / Lord: *Praise* Him and / magni-fy / Him for / ever.

[29] O ye servants of the *Lord* / bless ye the / Lord: *Praise* Him and / magni-fy / Him for / ever.

[30] O ye spirits and souls of the *righteous* / bless ye the / Lord: *Praise* Him and / magni-fy / Him for / ever.

[31] O ye holy and humble Men of *Heart* / bless Ye the / Lord: *Praise* Him and / magni-fy / Him for / ever.

[32] O Ananias and *Misael* / bless Ye the / Lord: *Praise* Him and / magni-fy / Him for / ever.

But there were four men who were there. If God wants to save you, God will save you. No power is equal to the power of God. God has put that same power in you if you are a true Christian.

Shadrach, Meshach, and Abednego were delivered by this same God. My brothers and sisters, do not fear native doctors or occultic people or witches and wizards. Don't fear them; they even fear you. They fear you. Why should you pack away for an occultic man? Who should pack away? He should pack out, of course, not you. You are insulting God if you pack away for an occultic man or if your church is here and an occultic man is in the church and you leave the church. No! This world belongs to our own God. This world belongs to God; nothing belongs to them. Why must you run away because of Satan's agents? The church is our Father's house and not theirs! See what the scripture says in Colossians 1:16–18:

> For by Him were all things created, that are in heaven, and that are in earth, visible and invisible, whether they be thrones, or dominions, or principalities, or powers: all things were created by Him, and for him: and He is before all things, and by Him all things consist.

And Colossians 2:9–10 buttresses this sacred fact.

> For in Him dwelleth all the fullness of the Godhead bodily. And ye are complete in Him, which is the head of all principality and power.

Many years ago, in Port Harcourt, Nigeria, a little boy was preaching in a bus, and one occultic man told him, 'My boy, here no be church. Here na bus' (meaning 'This is not a church. Stop preaching here'). The boy continued talking about Jesus, and that occultic man got angry—very, very angry. He said, 'I am telling you, stop disturbing us. Here na bus. No be church.' The boy continued preaching, and the occultic man became wild and said, 'I command you, boy, get naked. You no dey hear something, get naked' (meaning 'You are stubborn'). The boy started undressing in the bus there and then. The boy was getting mad. It was serious. The boy was seen removing his dress inside the bus. But there was a Christian brother in that bus who was not even of the same denomination as the boy. He said, 'I can't be here while Christ is insulted. They are insulting Jesus Christ.' No matter the church you attend, we have one Christ. Whether you are a member of the Assemblies of God Church or a Methodist or an Anglican, it does not matter. All Christians are of one gene—the Holy Spirit! They are like us; they worship the same God as we do. So that Christian brother got angry and said, 'In the name of Jesus, you, boy, put on your dress.' That boy started putting on his dress. The Christian brother turned to the occultic man and said, 'I command you, remove your own dress.' The occultic man started removing his dress there in the public. When somebody is insulting a member of the Deeper Life Church, for instance, don't say it doesn't concern you; it concerns you. He is a Christian brother. Hallelujah!

Christians should know that our God is awesome and His power is all-surpassing. A church invited an evangelist for a four-day revival meeting on Thursday, Friday, Saturday, and Sunday. On the first day of the programme, the visiting preacher preached, and at the end of his programme, a woman went to him and said, 'Pastor, please pray for me.' The pastor asked the woman why she needed prayers. The woman said, *'Every night, if I open my body now, you will run. Every night, them dey tear my body.* (meaning 'Every night, witches and wizards make marks on my body).' The pastor asked her, 'Are you a Christian?' She said yes. He said, 'I will not pray for you. You are a Christian, and they are tearing your body. What did you do?' This woman left, and she was crying and groaning. She went back to her house, knelt by her bed, and cried. 'God, what have I done? You have abandoned me. Your minister has refused to pray for me. What have I done?' She fell asleep on her knees by the bed while she was crying. She woke up the following morning. Nothing had happened to her. There were no marks of witchcraft on her body. She was surprised.

On Friday, the second day of the programme, she came to the revival meeting again and went back home and slept on her bed. They did not tear her body again. On the third day, Saturday, she went again to the revival meeting, and nothing happened to her. They didn't tear her body. In the early hours of Sunday, another woman knocked at her door and said, 'Madam, madam, I want to follow you to that place you are going.' She said okay and gave her a rundown of the programme of her church: 'Our Sunday school starts by 8 a.m. Come by at 8 a.m. The main service will start by 10 a.m.' The woman came, and they went together. After Sunday school, during the question-and-answer session, this woman put up her hand to ask a question. The pastor refused because he didn't know her. That woman was not a member.

In the seventies, the practice in the Assemblies of God Church was that unless you were their member, they would not regard you as a believer. They believed that without being a registered member of their church, you did not have the Holy Spirit. If you told them that you needed to be filled with the Holy Spirit, they would tell you, 'Come to our church. Otherwise, you will not have the Holy Spirit.' This woman put her hand up, but the pastor refused to allow her to ask questions. However, on the insistence of the visiting evangelist who preached at the revival, the woman came forward and beckoned to the woman who had suffered the ordeal of her body being torn every night, to follow her in facing the congregation. She said, '*Na me dey tear this woman body every night, na me. But I go there on Thursday night. She was kneeling by her bed, and fire surrounded her. I couldn't tear her body. I said this woman, so this woman don go make juju, I go kill am on Friday, I go finish am. So on Friday, I went to tear her body, and fire surrounded the whole bed. I couldn't go to her. I said, "Wonderful. This woman don go make juju." On Saturday, I go finish am. I come Saturday. I couldn't enter the house. Fire everywhere. Fire, fire everywhere. So I want to know where this woman is getting her power from. I know no say na Jesus dey give am this power, so from today I'll give my life to Jesus.*'

I am not saying that these satanic agents don't have power, but I am referring to the power that is above their own power—the power of God, which has pre-eminence over all things.

Apparently, the witch was saying that she was the person who paid the Christian woman evil nocturnal visits to suck her blood. On Thursday night, when the witch went to suck her blood, the woman was kneeling by her bed but was surrounded by fire. The witch vowed to deal with the woman on Friday. But when the witch went into her room on Friday night, the woman was sleeping comfortably with fire surrounding her. On Saturday night, the witch was unable to carry out her enterprise because she could not enter the room. Fire filled the entire room, and the Christian woman was sleeping. The witch eventually gave her life to Christ. She confessed that the power protecting that Christian woman was superior to her own witchcraft powers. That superior power is in Christ Jesus! He is the King of kings and the Lord of lords, the Alpha and Omega, the Beginning and the End, the First and Last, the Holy One of Israel, the Lion of the tribe of Judah, the Mighty Healer, the Mighty Deliverer, the Power of God. Hallelujah.

> Lyric: I love my Jesus. My Jesus loves me. No circumstances can change my decision. (3×)

There was a woman whom my mother entrusted to take care of me when I was a little boy. I used to go to her house to eat. One day, she called on me and asked my wife, Beatrice, to be present. She told us, 'When you were a small boy, you know, your mother gave you to me. You used to come to my house and eat. Now you are a big man. You are a pastor now. I am begging you, please. Get lost. Go and fend for yourself. You can go to Ogoni and "cook" yourself (fortify yourself with charms), or Benin, or go to Calabar and "cook" yourself so that they will not kill you. I am begging you, my son.' I couldn't imagine myself, God's servant, a servant of the Most High would go to God's enemy.the devil, to protect me. Imagine that! However, I thanked the woman for her misplaced concern and love for us and referred her to what the Bible says in *Psalm 91:1–16.*

> [1] He that dwelleth in the secret place of the most High shall abide under the shadow of the Almighty.

2 I will say of the Lord, He is my refuge and my fortress: my God; in Him will I trust.

3 Surely, He shall deliver thee from the snare of the fowler, and from the noisome pestilence.

4 He shall cover thee with His feathers, and under His wings shalt thou trust: His truth shall be thy shield and buckler.

5 Thou shalt not be afraid for the terror by night; nor for the arrow that flieth by day;

6 Nor for the pestilence that walketh in darkness; nor for the destruction that wasteth at noonday.

7 A thousand shall fall at thy side, and ten thousand at thy right hand; but it shall not come nigh thee.

8 Only with thine eyes shalt thou behold and see the reward of the wicked.

9 Because thou hast made the Lord, which is my refuge, even the most High, thy habitation;

10 There shall no evil befall thee, neither shall any plague come nigh thy dwelling.

11 For He shall give His angels charge over thee, to keep thee in all thy ways.

12 They shall bear thee up in their hands, lest thou dash thy foot against a stone.

[13] Thou shalt tread upon the lion and adder: the young lion and the dragon shalt thou trample under feet.

[14] Because He hath set His love upon me, therefore will I deliver him: I will set him on high, because He hath known my name.

[15] He shall call upon me, and I will answer him: I will be with him in trouble; I will deliver him, and honour him.

[16] With long life will I satisfy him, and shew him my salvation.

This scripture remains the heritage of any believer in Christ.

Again, Psalm 125 says:

[1] They that trust in the Lord shall be as mount Zion, which cannot be removed, but abideth for ever.

[2] As the mountains are round about Jerusalem, so the Lord is round about His people from henceforth even for ever.

[3] For the rod of the wicked shall not rest upon the lot of the righteous; lest the righteous put forth their hands unto iniquity.

[4] Do good, O Lord, unto those that be good, and to them that are upright in their hearts.

⁵ As for such as turn aside unto their crooked ways,
the Lord shall lead them forth with the workers of
iniquity: but peace shall be upon Israel.

I told you earlier that the whole of Nigeria is now under my control because of my position as Dean of the Church of Nigeria. So all the charms, all the witches in the whole of Nigeria, all the cult members, and all the native doctors are under my control! Can you please clap for Jesus Christ?

> Chorus: Jesus na You be Oga, Jesus na You be
> Oga. Every other god na so so yeye, every
> other god na so so mumu. (2×)

Can you clap for Jesus Christ?

Did you know that even when you are dreaming, when you mention the name of Jesus Christ, the devil will run away? How much more in person? The Bible says that at the mention of Jesus, every knee must bow. Proverbs 18:10 says, 'The name of the Lord is a strong tower, the righteous hide in the name and they are safe.' I am safe in the name of Jesus.

If you hide yourself in that name, you are safe. The Psalm of David reaffirms our safety and protection with these words: 'The Lord is my shepherd I shall not want, He makes me lie down in green pastures. He leads me beside the still waters, He restoreth my soul. He leads me in the paths of righteousness for His name sake, ye though I walk through the valley of the shadow of death, I will fear no evil: for thou art with me; thy rod and thy staff they comfort me. Thou preparest a table before me in the presence of mine enemies: thou anointest my head with oil; my cup runneth over. Surely goodness and mercy shall follow me all the days of my life: and I shall dwell in the house of the Lord forever.' The Lord God Almighty did not give a limited time frame within which His goodness and mercy would follow us; it is for all the days of our lives. Can you clap for Jesus?

Recall again that the pagan king said, 'Blessed be the God of Shadrach, Meshach, and Abednego.' The king resorted to praising another man's God, leaving his own god and his image. I am sure he must have thrown away that god after some time. How can you leave the only true God and worship fake gods? The Bible says that God has given Jesus a name above every other name; that at the name of Jesus, every knee must bow, whether in heaven or on earth; and that every tongue must confess that Jesus Christ is Lord, to the glory of God. Look at the heathen king praising our own God, yet we leave our God to go and worship another god. There are people who have charms, while some others leave satanic marks on their bodies to wade off evil spirits, popularly known as *ogbanje* in some cultures. Why would you make a mark on your body so that *ogbanje* would not see you, when you can just say a word and any evil spell or enchantment will disappear?

There was a church some years ago, when this diocese was under the Niger Delta Diocese. The Bishop then (the late Papa Elenwo) posted a pastor to one of the churches, while another pastor was to leave the church. That pastor refused to leave the church. That time, it was a district with many churches supervised by one pastor. The pastor refused to leave the church, until the Bishop forced him out. But before he left the church, he went to a native doctor who prepared a charm he kept inside the parsonage. (This happened about thirty years ago.) He put juju inside the parsonage. I am sure no pastor can do that now. Today it is a common experience to see fellow pastors criticise one another and carry out smear campaigns, one against the other. Some pastors, when they are transferred out of a parish, will tell those they are leaving behind, 'The pastor posted to you is not a good man,' just to poison the minds of the parishioners.

The incoming pastor will tell the same parishioners, 'The pastor who has just been transferred has spoilt the church. I will commence rebuilding it.' That is what pastors do. The person going will condemn the one coming, and the one coming will condemn the one going.

The outgoing pastor made juju and kept it in the parsonage and said, 'Let me see who will come to this place and replace me.' The incoming pastor barely stayed in the parsonage for one month before he packed out in fear, in preference for a rented house in the village. When the Parish Church Council (PCC) held a meeting, he was not there. The church congregation got embarrassed for the reason that all the people knew that the pastor was not staying in the parsonage. They went and consulted a native doctor. See, those people who are Christians today should be grateful to God. In the early days, you could not say you were born-again. A juju priest at that time would come to the harvest with about four or five wives, and while dancing, a pastor would bless him with his goat, beer, and palm wine.

In PCC meetings, members were at liberty to drink palm wine and smoke cigarettes. A man who was the bell-ringer at the time was notoriously seen publicly with his cigarettes and snuff. When the pastor packed out of the parsonage, the PCC went and called a native doctor to come and 'cleanse' the parsonage for them. You can imagine that nonsense; they used church money to bring in a native doctor. So the native doctor came, and after he had used the blood of goat and fowl to perform rituals, the incoming pastor now found pleasure and relief to pack into the parsonage. Today it would only require a little girl undertaking fasting and prayer and the blood of the Lamb to cleanse the vicarage spiritually. We have power, but we don't know the power God has given to us by just speaking the word. How can a PCC consult and call a native doctor, Satan's priest, to come and cleanse a church environment? What type of church is that? Is it Christ's church or Satan's church?

My brothers and sisters, our God is the only true God. There is no god above this God.

Tonight we shall see the power of God. Tonight your life will turn around again. I don't know how many years you have been barren; I don't know. Only God knows. I don't know how many people have proposed marriage to you and then disappointed you. There are beautiful girls whom suitors go to for marriage, but after two months, the suitors withdraw. However, tonight we shall break that yoke! We shall break that yoke; I said all powers are under my control, so I will reverse every power working against you. People are wicked; people are very, very wicked. There are people out there who neither go to consult juju nor elect to serve God but who are in the choir. They like singing, but they are not serving God. They like prayers, but they are not Christians.

Give your life to Christ first. When you give your life to Christ, the Holy Spirit will come into your life and dwell inside you. When wicked and diabolic people attack you, they will not get you, because the Holy Ghost will be your advocate; He will be your lawyer—that is His work. He won't let you down. God will never let you down. King David said, 'The Lord is my Light and my Salvation, whom shall I fear? The Lord is the Stronghold of my life, of whom shall I be afraid?' (Psalm 27:1–2). If you are a Christian or a believer, not necessarily confirmed or baptised, you may be a knight or lay reader, because you can be a lay reader yet not a Christian. I plead passionately that you give your life to Christ. Can you allow God to control your life, your whole system? Let us pray.

> Prayer: The Lord God of Shadrach, Meshach, and Abednego, we thank You for Your incomprehensible, comprehensive, and indomitable power in the life of Your people. We thank You because You never disappoint those who put their trust in You.

We pray, by the power of Your Holy Spirit, enable us to put our trust and confidence in You and You alone and to reject all the false attractions of the devil through Jesus Christ our Lord. Amen.

3

DAY 3

'And Moses said to the people, "Do not be afraid. Stand still and see the salvation of the Lord, which shall be accomplished for you today, for the Egyptians whom you are seeing today you shall see no more forever. The Lord shall fight for you and you shall hold your peace"' (Exodus 14:13–14). Tell yourself, 'The Lord shall fight for me.'

There are two persons who can fight for you. Either the devil will fight for you, or God will fight for you, depending on the choice you make between the two. When you consult native doctors and juju priests, you are asking the devil to fight for you, but when you go into prayer, looking up to heaven in faith, you are asking God to fight for you. I am sure you know what I am saying—that if you allow God to fight for you, you will be free. If you consult the devil to fight for you, then you are in trouble.

The theme of my message tonight is 'The Lord will fight for you'. This Lord God, who is God, the Master of the whole universe, the King of kings and Lord of lords, the Alpha and Omega, the only true God, and the God of Elijah, will fight for you in Jesus's name. Amen.

If you want to harm yourself, go and fight a child of God. If you want trouble, go and touch a child of God. It is dangerous for anyone to fight a true Christian. John says, 'As many as received Him He gave them authority to become children of God' (John 1:12). When you give your life to Jesus Christ, God adopts you into His family, and that is what it means. When you are in the family of God, God will take care of you.

The Israelites have been God's chosen people from the beginning. Without any apology, God told Moses, 'You shall say to Pharaoh, "Thus says the LORD: Israel is My son, My firstborn."' The place of Israel in God's mandate under heaven is rightly situated in God's promise to Abram in a vision, when He said, 'Do not be afraid, Abram. I am your shield, your exceedingly great reward' (Genesis 15:1). At this time, Abram, as he was then known, had no child by Sarai, his barren wife. Abraham and Sarah trusted and believed God when He assured them of being their 'exceedingly great reward'. Abraham, however, expressed reservations with that promise when he replied to God: 'Lord God, what will you give me, seeing I go childless, and the heir of my house is Eliezer of Damascus?' (Genesis 15:2). The Lord God said to him, 'This one shall not be your heir, but one who will come from your own body shall be your heir' (Genesis 15:4). In reaffirming His promise to Abraham, God brought him outside and urged him to look towards heaven and count the stars to see if he could number them, all to assure Abraham of the exceedingly great reward of His descendants being like the stars of heaven. The scripture recorded that Abraham believed God, and He accounted it to him for righteousness (Genesis 15:6). It is to be noted that *believing God* and *believing in God* are not one and the same thing. One may believe God exists but may not take God at His Word.

Sarah, in due time, bore a son, Isaac.

Meanwhile, in another encounter with God, Abraham was put in a deep sleep. God revealed to Abraham how his descendants would be strangers in a land that was not theirs and would remain in servitude and be afflicted for 400 years. But the entire story of Israel's bondage in Egypt changed when God called Moses out of the midst of his people to lead them out of Egypt. Moses's onerous call through the burning-bush encounter was not without trials, and his travails came to a head when he killed an Egyptian who had been quarrelling with a Hebrew. He left Egypt and took refuge in Midian. Earlier, Moses had doubted his ability to take up the mantle to lead the children of Israel out of Egypt, for he complained to God about his disability, being a stammerer. The Lord's anger was kindled against him when he said, 'O my Lord, please send by the hand of whomever else you may send' (Exodus 4:13). God preferred Moses rather than Aaron, his elder brother and priest, and He told Moses, 'Is not Aaron the Levite your brother? I know that he can speak well . . . So he shall be your spokesman to the people. And he himself shall be as mouth for you and you shall be to him as God' (Exodus 4:14–16). Let us hear God's authority to Moses: 'So the LORD said to Moses, "See, I have made you as God to Pharaoh, and Aaron your brother shall be your prophet"' (Exodus 7:1).

God said in Exodus 4:22–23, 'Then you shall say to Pharaoh, "Thus says the Lord, Israel is My son, My firstborn. So, I say to you, let My son go that they may serve Me but if you refuse them to go, indeed I will kill your first son, your first born'. Did God not do it? God did it. So if you are a child of God, it is God's responsibility to take care of you. Christ said, 'If you who are evil know how to give gifts to your children, how much more will your heavenly Father give you good things?' If you have a child, no matter how bad that child is, you will still feed the child. You can't do without the child. How much more your heavenly Father? God said, 'Israel is my firstborn. If you don't let him go and worship me in the wilderness, I will kill your firstborn,' and God did it. Up to the present day, Israel is still God's firstborn. God cannot change His promise to Israel.

All the countries surrounding them are enemies, namely, Iran, Iraq, Jordan, Syria, and Lebanon. Israel is a country of about six million people, but nobody can defeat them, because Israel is God's firstborn. Though surrounded by enemies, Israel has never been defeated by her contemporary foes. So if you are God's child, God's business is to take care of you. God will assign His angels to watch over you. You don't need any other help.

So Moses led the people of Israel out of Egypt. Don't forget that the Israelites had no army at the time. They were refugees, slaves in Egypt. When they were going, they were going with their children, their wives, and their old men and old women. They were going, and Pharaoh decided to pursue them. He mobilised his army to pursue them, and it reached the point that the people of Israel were trapped between the Red Sea and Pharaoh's army, which was in hot pursuit. But God was ready to fight for them, and that is how God will fight for you, in Jesus's name. Amen.

They got trapped; the Red Sea was in front, and by the right and left were mountains. They were 600,000 people, besides children and women. The multitude of Israel could have been slaughtered, but Moses was with them. It is indeed good to have strong leaders. Aware that Pharaoh and his army were pursuing them, the people started complaining to Moses.

They murmured and said, 'Is this not the word that we spoke to you in Egypt, "Let us alone that we may serve the Egyptians?" It would have been better to serve the Egyptians than to die in the wilderness' (Exodus 14:12). They were all afraid, but see what Moses said: 'Do not be afraid, stand still and see the salvation of the Lord which He will accomplish for you. But the Egyptians which you see today, you shall see them no more and forever.'

'The Lord shall fight for you, and you will hold your peace' is a prophetic proclamation. Moses gave them the assurance that God would fight for them. They had no army; God of the army of Israel fought for them. When the man who replaced Moses, Joshua, was about to take possession of Jericho, as usual he went to a quiet place to pray. As he was praying, he saw a man with a drawn sword. He asked the man, 'Are you for us or against us?' The man said, 'No, but as Commander-in-chief of the army of God, I have come.' That man was Jesus Christ. Jesus said, 'Before Abraham was, I am.' He was the man whom Nebuchadnezzar saw in the burning furnace—the fourth man. The testimony of John the Baptist about how Jesus Christ has pre-eminence in all things in creation and is himself the beginning, is as written in John 1:1–3: 'In the beginning was the word and the word was with God and the word was God. All things were made by Him and without Him was not anything made that was made.'

John further said that in Him was the light of men. Verse 14 says, 'And the Word became flesh and dwell among us and we beheld His glory as of the only begotten [that Son was Jesus Christ].' He was from the beginning. The same Christ appeared to Joshua and said, 'As the commander-in-chief of the army of God, I have come.' He commanded Joshua to march around the walls of Jericho seven times for seven days, and then the place would collapse. Joshua did that, and the walls of Jericho came down flat.

God's angels are always ready to help us if we are living a holy, cleansed life. If you are not living a holy life, you are on your own. As a child of God, you always have God's angels beside you to protect you. If you go to native doctors, Satan's angels are there to protect you also. So it depends who protects you. Everybody has either God's angels or the devil's angels to protect him or her.

Many years ago, in one of the open-air crusades I organised when I was pastor at Saint John's Anglican Church, Rumueme, in Rivers State, an old woman called me aside and bore witness to how she saw twelve angels wearing white apparel following me as I climbed the podium to introduce the guest speaker. That was moments after I introduced the guest speaker. She had called me and said, 'Pastor, come.' I went, and she said, 'Una plenty oooo' (meaning 'You people are many'). I did not understand. She knew I didn't understand her, so she explained further: 'I saw twelve angels wearing white following you up the podium.' The truth is that although I did not see anybody while I climbed up and down the crusade podium, God had opened the eyes of the old woman to let her see me climb up and down in the company of His angels.

So as a child of God, at all times, be sure that you are well protected. Some people may doubt this sacred truth. However, it is only for you and for me, who truly believe. Some of you are greater vessels in God's hands. If God can protect me, why can't God protect you? Some of you spend hours in prayers and fasting. You are therefore God's chosen vessels and are under His watch day and night. If your hands are in dirty things, you cannot be guaranteed His protection. If you are living an uncleansed life of fornication and adultery and do all sorts of things, forget about it. God is not bound to protect you, because your life and the walls around you are porous. But if you are living a holy life, God has no reason not to protect you.

So Moses reassured the people that 'the Lord will fight for you, hold your peace'. God was angry with Moses, and I will tell you why He was angry with him. God told Moses, 'Why do you cry to me? Tell them to go forward. Lift your rod and stretch out your hand over the sea and divide the sea.' Why was God angry with Moses? It was because He had given Moses so much authority. Exodus 7:1 states,

> The Lord said to Moses see, I have made you a
> God to Pharaoh and Aaron your brother shall be
> your Prophet.

Do you know what it means when you are made *god* over somebody? That means you can control the person and all aspects of his or her life. Unfortunately, Moses could not utilise this God-given authority, the unlimited authority. Rather, sometimes he would cry, worried, and go back to God when faced with problems.

In Luke 10:19, my Lord Jesus said, '[Kattey], I have given you authority to tread upon serpents, and scorpions, upon all the powers of the enemy and nothing shall by any means hurt you' (the words in brackets are mine). Why don't you believe in what Christ said?

Paul said, 'If God be for you, who can be against you?' (Romans 8:31).

King Solomon said, 'The name of the Lord is a strong tower. The righteous hide in Him, and they are saved.'

Why can't we run to Christ and be saved? God's promises in His written Word (the Bible) are sure.

If God said that no weapon fashioned against you shall prosper, it remains a sure promise (Isaiah 54:17). If Moses failed to exercise that authority, he could have failed when the hour of deliverance came at the Red Sea.

God hardened the heart of Pharaoh, and his army pursued them. The reason God hardened Pharaoh's heart was to gain glory over the Egyptian king and his army and chariots. The Israelites, on the contrary, had no army, as we noted earlier. They were leaving the land of Egypt with their cattle, their children, and the gold rings and necklaces they collected as favour from the Egyptians.

It seemed an irony of some sort that the same God who had heard the cry of His people in bondage and raised a vessel in Moses to deliver them had hardened Pharaoh's heart so he would not let His people go. But thesoverign Lord chose to harden the heart of Pharaoh apparently to gain honour for himself over Pharaoh and his chariots and horsemen. The Lord God Almighty also proved himself to be sovereign by those plagues and the parting of a mighty ocean, the Red Sea, leaving the Israelites in no doubt that He is King of kings and Lord of lords. By the miraculous signs and wonders of the pillar of cloud that separated His people, Israel, and His enemies, the Egyptians, He justified His divinity and, indeed, the fact that He is the only true God.

Many people today do not know who God is. God is not like air; God is a personality. He has billions of angels, and it was only one angel that destroyed Sodom and Gomorrah. Only one single angel had to be assigned to slaughter a whole city or country in one night. God's power cannot be compared with any other power.

Moses led the people of Israel by night and by day. The Bible said, 'God told Moses to stretch forth the rod in his hand toward the Red Sea and the Lord caused the sea to go back by a strong east wind all that night, and made the sea into dry land, and the waters were divided' (Exodus 14:21). And they started moving—not one person, not two persons, not three persons, not four persons, but 600,000 persons. Moses was patient with them, and they crossed the Red Sea. When Moses went across the Red Sea, God removed the daylight. The Egyptians moved into the Red Sea, hoping to recover their captives. What happened? Moses removed the rod, and all the Egyptians drowned in the Red Sea. That is what God will do to your enemies also. Amen. God will drown your enemies in the Red Sea, in Jesus's name. Amen. See the song they sang at the wake of their deliverance from the bondage of the Egyptians:

Exodus 15:1 states

I will sing unto the Lord
For He has triumphed gloriously
The horse and the rider
He has thrown into the sea

This is its modern equivalent:

We are victorious, yes we are victorious
Glory be to God who has given us victory

That was how God fought for those who had no weapons. Our God is the help of the helpless. Our God is the hope of the hopeless. When you don't have any hope at all, God becomes your hope. My brothers and my sisters, I don't know what you are going through in life. I don't know how many enemies you have in life; you may not even know them. Your own best friend can be your worst enemy. Let me say it again: your own best friend can be your worst enemy.

In the 1940s, there was a famous trader who would go from place to place, but on Sundays, he made sure he never sold his hardware. He would go to church and return to his house. He became widely known, travelling with his goods, and became very wealthy. His own best friend started envying him and planned to kill him. Unknown to him, his best friend went to a native doctor to find a way to kill him. It is a common experience. The native doctor brought a basin of water and invoked in the water the spirit of the man. It is not difficult to kill anybody if you are not a Christian. They will invoke you in the water and kill you there or tell you what to do there. They can resort to invoking you to appear in the mirror and tell you what to do or poison you there, or they can stab you to death in your deep sleep. Some people, you may have heard, die in their sleep. Nobody can claim to have control of himself or herself in deep slumber. A person can be poisoned while sleeping, or something catastrophic can befall a person. But I am comforted that my God, Yahweh, the God of Israel, 'neither slumbers nor sleeps' (Psalms 121:4).

So when the native doctor brought a basin of water and invoked the trader's spirit in the water, the man appeared. To the native doctor's astonishment, he saw two men wearing white apparel beside the man—undoubtedly angels on a rescue mission. The native doctor told the disappointed friend of the trader, who witnessed the unfolding event, that unless the men (the angels) guiding his friend left him, it was impossible to kill him. The trader's friend was angry and could not accept that his friend had more power than the native doctor. On the contrary, the native doctor suggested the devil's advocacy to the trader's friend, urging him to convince his friend to go to a native doctor as a way of separating him from the guiding angels and giving him a way to be killed with ease.

This friend went back to the trader and said, 'My friend, you are becoming wealthier now. People are envying you. Please go and meet a native doctor who will spiritually fortify you so that you will not die, because your envious enemies will kill you.' The man said, 'I'm not going. God will protect me.' But after several attempts by his friend, the trader succumbed.

When the trader's friend went back to the native doctor and told him the trader had gone to consult a native doctor, they invoked him in the water again, only to discover that the angels had left him. They quickly killed the trader.

If you are a Christian, God has set His angels to always guard you; you don't need any other person to help you. If God had not been my guard, I would have died a long time ago. If you are truly a Christian, God will protect you. He will fight for you. It is His business to fight for His own children. The way you take care of your own children here on earth, that is how God takes care of His own children. He will never abandon you. David said, 'I was young, and now I am old. I have never seen the Lord forsake those who worship Him. But if you take to two ways, you are here and there at the same time. There is no guarantee that God will protect you. There is nobody who serves this way that is protected.'

The Bible says that if God is for you, who can be against you? God is the ultimate. He is all-powerful. He rules this universe. I want to say it again and again: this universe belongs to God. If you are a child of God, you have the right to live in His world. Nobody can kick you out of His world unless you don't attach yourself to God. Nobody has the right to kill you if you are a child of God, because He is thesoverign Lord who created all things. It seems many Christians today do not believe He is God. We don't believe that this God has power to do anything. If indeed we believe it, we would never seek help from anywhere else. People join secret societies because they are afraid of what other people will do to them. I don't blame them.

But they have forgotten that there is Somebody who is supreme. Why would you go to a lesser god rather than the One who is above all things? He is called the Most High God.

Hear what Prophet Isaiah said:

> Behold, the nations of the world are as a drop in
> a bucket and are counted as the small dust on the
> scales. (Isaiah 40:15)

Then in verse 17, it says, 'All nations before Him are as nothing and they are counted to Him less than nothing, and vanity.'

What this implies is that all the nations of the earth—the United States of America, England, China, Russia, amongst others—are as nothing before God. He can destroy this world in a second. To the God who is backing you, who is behind you and beside you, the whole world is nothing before him. He can destroy this nation in a second. He will just speak a word; He doesn't even need to act before His desires are accomplished. That is the person I am telling you to cling to.

There is nothing this God cannot do. Jesus said, 'With men everything is impossible but with God all things are possible' (Mark 10:27).

In the Bible, the story of Hannah, the wife of Elkanah (1 Samuel 1:2), is well known to us. Hannah was a barren woman, and she spoke to this God. God gave her children. The account of Gideon, who fought 135,000 Midianite soldiers, is even more fascinating. When Gideon deployed 32,000 soldiers for Israel, God said they were too many. With only 300 soldiers, Gideon fought the Midianites and won. You don't need a large number; all you need is God behind you. If He is with you, no man can defeat you, no woman can defeat you, and no witch can take your fortune.

Did you know that somebody can change your fortune? While you are moving straight, somebody can go and make charms and spoil your way. But you see, as I am here now, if you invoke me in the mirror, the blood of Jesus will appear on my behalf, because I am a Christian. If you are a Christian, be sure that you are secured in the hand of Christ.

This God we are talking about will never change His style. This God is a God who loves the holiness of life. He wants you to trust Him. If you trust this God, you will never be disappointed. There is no one who ever trusted in this God and got disappointed. David was not disappointed; not even Daniel was disappointed. My brothers and my sisters, if there is nothing you've learnt in these three days, know that God is supreme and that whatsoever your aim is that is not of God, come out of it. Let God take over your matter; let God take over your situation. Don't listen to anybody who tells you to help yourself in any other way that is not of God. It is not in the Bible. It is often said that heaven helps those who help themselves. It is not in the Bible anywhere. So God wants those who will cling to Him and Him alone. God has assured those who put their trust in Him with the following words: 'I will go before you. And make the crooked places straight; I will break in pieces the gates of bronze, and cut the bars of iron. I will give you the treasures of darkness, and hidden riches of secret places, that you may know that I, the Lord, who call you by your name, Am the God of Israel' (Isaiah 45:2–3).

God will do much more for you if you allow Him direct your life. How do you become a Christian? It is simple: confess your sins and ask Christ to come into your life. You commit to it and ask Him to guide you by His Holy Spirit if you want to truly be His child and if you are sincere. Christ will come into your life, and your life will change. I am sure He is going to protect you.

Let us pray:

Sovereign Lord God, the God of Israel, we thank You for Your power to free people from the shackles of sin and the domination of the devil. We pray, Lord, in Your abundant mercy, release us all from all the powers that hold back our freedom. Arise, O God, and let Your enemies be scattered. May it please You, God of Moses, to give us victory day by day in situations and conditions that hold us in bondage. We ask this through the merit of Your Son, Jesus Christ, our Lord. Amen.

4

EXCERPTS FROM ARCHBISHOP'S ADDRESS AT UYO

These are excerpts of the Archbishop's address delivered at the provincial council held at Cathedral Church of All Saints, Uyo, Diocese of Uyo, on Wednesday, 4 September, 2013.

Your Lordships,
Our Provincial mother and Diocesan mothers,
Beloved Clergy and Laity,
People of God here present,

Greetings and welcome.
With great joy in our hearts and on behalf of Beatrice, my wife, and I, we welcome you to this meeting of the Province of Niger Delta in the name of our Lord and Saviour, Jesus Christ.

The Bishops, the clergy, and the lay delegates have shown great dedication to the work of this Province, and to that, we are very grateful. The Provincial Women President, Beatrice, and the Bishops' wives have also shown wonderful commitment to the work of women and the girl child in this province.

RECEPTION AND THANKSGIVING SERVICE

We use this medium to thank Rt Rev. Solomon Gberegbara (JP) and wife Stella, Bishop of the Diocese of Ogoni, for organising a super reception for us as Dean of the Church of Nigeria. This reception was widely televised. The crowd that lined the road at various points from Nonwa to Bori was unprecedented, with a convoy of over two hundred vehicles. Bori City came to a standstill. May God bless the Diocese of Ogoni.

The performance by the Diocese of Ogoni challenged the Diocese of Niger Delta North to completely take over the thanksgiving service of the Dean. The thanksgiving was proposed to be private and low-key, but the Diocese of Niger Delta North synod, having seen what the Diocese of Ogoni did, undertook to bankroll the thanksgiving service.

We use this opportunity to thank the Province of Niger Delta for attending the thanksgiving service.

The Diocese of Etche organised a very warm and touching reception service for us as Dean on Saturday, 24 August 2013. On Friday, 23 August 2013, which was my birthday, Bishop Nwala took us to pay courtesy call on HRH Eze Sir Dr Samuel Amaechi, Onye-Ishi Agwuru Igbo clan, and his wife, Leah. The council of chiefs of the clan were there to receive us with a birthday cake. Later, we paid a courtesy call on HRH Eze Sir Monday Ojiegbe, Onye-Ishi Agwuru Omuma clan, and his wife, with the council of chiefs. At the Palaces of the Royal Fathers, we were warmly received. May God bless them. We thank the Bishop Rt Rev.

Precious Nwala and wife, as well as all the faithful of the Diocese of Etche for such a great honour done us.

ANGLICAN CABLE NETWORK NIGERIA

For the first time in the history of the Church of Nigeria (Anglican Communion), we now have a cable network, thanks to the idea and innovation of the Primate, His Grace, Most Reverend Nicholas Okoh. It is now on test transmission on My TV Channel.

JOINT COUNCIL OF PROVINCES EAST OF THE NIGER

As you know, this province is part of the Joint Council of Provinces East of the Niger, the former Province II. We have three main institutions that bring us together. They are Paul University Awka, Trinity Theological College Umuahia, and Superannuation Fund.

i.   **Paul University Awka**

The Chairman, Board of Trustees is Dr Alex Ekwueme. Efforts are being made to appoint the chairman of the council.

The Vice-Chancellor is Prof. G. Igboeli, who is making a lot of sacrifices to ensure the university takes its appropriate place in the comity of universities.

The NUC is coming for accreditation in October 2013, and we plead with all dioceses to pay their debts and obligations to enable us to have a smooth accreditation. Payments should be made to Province II Anglican Communion, Joint Council of East Provinces Account No. 0035652154 with Union Bank.

Each diocese is allocated twenty chances for student admission this year. Every diocese should please endeavour to fill up the twenty vacancies allocated to it.

ii. Trinity Theological College Umuahia

The chairman of the council, Rt Rev. David Onuoha, with zeal and dedication, is working with the council to ensure that the hostel being built is completed in time. All past students of Trinity Theological College are to pay the sum of one thousand naira (₦1,000) every month for three years, for the purpose of completing the hostel project. His Grace, the Most Reverend Nicholas Okoh, has been invited to lay the stone of the hostel building on 9 September 2013. All the dioceses east of the Niger are to be represented at this ceremony.

iii. Superannuation Fund

Every clergy and church worker in the provinces and dioceses east of the Niger has been a contributor to this fund since 1948. If there is any diocese whose clergy is not a contributor, that diocese is to be blamed. Our clergy needs to retire with some basic care. We plead with legal officers, synod secretaries, financial secretaries, Bishops' chaplains, etc. to remind their Bishops about remittance to this fund. Anyone not contributing to this fund is doing himself or herself great harm in the future. If anyone is in doubt about this fund, you may contact Mr Humphrey Amadi, who is versed in the superannuation affairs, for details.

STANDING COMMITTEE

As we all know, the standing committee of the Church of Nigeria (Anglican Communion) will be hosted by the Province of Niger Delta at the Diocese of Niger Delta West from 9 to 14 September 2013.

We thank the Rt Rev. Emmanuel Oko-Jaja, his wife, and all the faithful in the diocese for the arrangements they have put in place for the meeting. We must appreciate the financial and moral support of the dioceses of this province given to the Diocese of Niger Delta West. All the dioceses were levied not to support but as hosts to the meeting. Bishop Oko-Jaja will give us a detailed report in the course of this meeting, and we request him to state clearly the dioceses that have not paid their levies.

On Tuesday, 10 September 2013, there will be consecration of Very Reverend Titus Olayinka as Bishop of Ogbomosho.

We must continue to pray for this meeting and for the Primate of all Nigeria, His Grace, the Most Reverend Nicholas Okoh, that God would endow him with wisdom.

THE CRISIS IN NIGERIA/RIVERS STATE

The ongoing crisis in Nigeria, which has its fulcrum in Rivers State, is unfortunate. That two friends (who could not do without each other and who helped themselves to rise to the top) could not agree is more unfortunate. The crisis *seems* to be insignificant. That was how the Western crisis in 1964–1966 started and grew into a full-blown civil war that took away many lives.

Up until now, none of them have told us the real problem that has caused the crisis. Unfortunately, people have taken sides, and rather than help to resolve the problem, they are worsening it. It now involves the President, the first lady, and the political party. The crisis has definitely divided the country into two factions: those supporting Governor Chibuike Amaechi and those supporting the Honourable Minister of State for Education, President Goodluck Jonathan, and his wife, Dame Patience.

No matter the denial, the presidency is neck-deep in the crisis. If the President wants to end it today, the whole crisis will end. But this crisis cannot be resolved by delegations going to the President and blackmailing Governor Amaechi or by delegations visiting the governor to blackmail the President, his wife, and Hon. Nyesom Wike. Nor will the crisis be resolved by making statements that annoy the other side of the divide.

The Democratic Republic of Congo has not recovered from a similar crisis that has engulfed the country since 1960. Patrice Lumumba and Moise Tshombe had a quarrel, and until today, Zaire or the Congo have known no peace since 1960. Though Patrice Lumumba was killed, Moise Tshombe died a natural death. The Congo crisis led to the death of the then UN secretary-general Dag Hammarskjöld in a controversial air crash.

Somalia, since 1989, has not recovered from their crisis until now. Let the political class resolve their crisis. They know what to do to resolve the crisis. This country does not belong to the political class only; it belongs to all of us: lawyers, doctors, teachers, engineers, the military, the police, the clergy, and people of all professions. The political class should not put this country into chaos. The note of warning is this: *all the parties may in the end lose out, unless they find definite ways of resolving the conflict.*

Theme: 'The Lord, He is God! The Lord, He is God.'

The theme for this Council Meeting is 'The LORD, He is God! The LORD, He is God' (1 Kings 18:38–39).

The Israel of God was in a mess. They were deeply involved in idolatry and worship of Baal. King Ahab married Jezebel, who brought with her the god of her nation, Sidon. Hear God's assessment of Ahab:

> And Ahab the son of Omri did evil in the sight of the Lord above all that were before him. And it came to pass, as if it had been a light thing for him to walk in the sins of Jeroboam the son of Nebat, that he took to wife Jezebel the daughter of Ethbaal king of the Zidonians, and went and served Baal, and worshipped him. And he reared up an altar for Baal in the house of Baal, which he had built in Samaria. And Ahab made a grove; and Ahab did more to provoke the Lord God of Israel to anger than all the kings of Israel that were before him. (1 Kings 16:30–33)

Everybody did what the king did. As a result of King Ahab and Queen Jezebel's worship of Baal, the worship of Baal became a state religion. The situation was so bad that true worshippers either went into hiding or had to pretend they were also worshipping Ahab's Baal in God's chosen nation, Israel.

In every nation, state, town, or village, when things are going contrary, God always raises up a man or woman whom perhaps others may not understand, but God's finger is on him or her.

When all Israel was in bondage in Egypt, God raised Moses to deliver them. When all Israel was to be slaughtered by haughty Haman, God raised beautiful Queen Esther and her cousin Mordecai to save His people, Israel. When the Midianites vowed that Israel should not exist as a people, God raised Gideon, who, with only 300 ragtag soldiers, under God routed and defeated 135,000 soldiers of the Midianites.

In the time of Ahab, God raised Elijah the Prophet, who challenged Ahab and Jezebel and sought to correct the anomalies in the worship life of Israel. Elijah summoned all Israel and Ahab to Mount Carmel and threw this challenge:

How long will you falter between two opinions?
If the Lord is God, follow Him; but if Baal, follow
him. (1 Kings 18:212)

The nature of the fallen man is to be double-faced. A man has an official wife known to everyone. Then he must also want to have unofficial wives elsewhere, unknown to others. Some have Jehovah as their official God but have other gods as well. There are many in the church who have their native gods as their official god but Jehovah as their unofficial god and vice versa. Such are part-time worshippers of Jehovah.

The government, a secular institution, is against membership of secret cults and societies. Is it not unfortunate that the church, which should join the government in championing this crusade, still has some of her members in secret societies and cults?

How long will we go limping between two opinions?
Then the context. This can be read from 1 Kings 18. No doubt, the Lord our God won. Then the people of Israel prostrated themselves on the ground, shouting:

> The LORD, He is God!
> The LORD, He is God!

Our God is always victorious. He never loses a battle or war. He is always triumphant, always a winner.

> He is a mighty man in battle
> El Shaddai
> He is a mighty man in battle
> Jehovah Nisi
> He is a mighty man in battle
> El Shaddai
> He is a mighty man in battle

Glory to His name.

The true God is not a nameless God. His name is Jehovah. He is the Creator. He is a real personality—not a lifeless natural law operating, not a blind force working through a series of accidents and coincidences to develop one thing or another.

The true God is a Supreme Being, self-existent, self-sufficient, eternal, sovereign, absolutely free, and all-powerful.

The LORD, He is God! The LORD, He is God!
Do you really know this God?
Do you know His only begotten Son, Jesus Christ?
Have you allowed yourself to be led and directed by His Holy Spirit?
May God draw us closer to him, in Jesus's name. Amen.

And now unto Him who is able to do exceedingly abundantly above all we ask or think, according to the power that works in us. To Him be glory in the church by Christ Jesus to all generations. To Him be dominion, power, and majesty now and forever and evermore. Amen.

God bless you all.

5

THE JOURNEY THAT LED TO THE KIDNAP

My wife, Beatrice; my chaplain, Rev. Romauld Foko; my driver, Eric; and I left Uyo on Thursday.

During the meeting, I told the Bishops I would be at Yenagoa to inspect the facilities and ascertain the level of preparations for the Church of Nigeria standing committee meeting that would be held the following week, from 9 to 14 September 2013. The Bishops offered to join me at Yenagoa, the administrative headquarters of the Diocese of Niger Delta West.

The Bishop, Rt Rev. Emmanuel Oko-jaja, and wife had mobilised the faithful in Niger Delta West to make preparation for the hosting of the standing committee meeting. In the company of my wife, the Bishops of the Province of Niger Delta (some came with their wives) and I travelled to Yenagoa. It was a successful trip. We went round to see the level of preparations made, and we made useful suggestions. On our way to that journey, my friend Ven. Dr S. T. K. Appah called me to tell me he was expecting to see me during the standing committee meeting. After the incident, he reminded me that I told him, 'By the grace of God,' and that struck him. *'By the grace of God'? What does the Dean mean by that?* he asked himself.

There were three remarkable incidents that took place on the day of the inspection at Yenagoa. Let me mention two of them. During the inspection of the venue for feeding the delegates, the host Bishop told us that food would be prepared at a different venue, at another church compound a few kilometres away from Saint Peter's Church, Yenagoa. I observed that it might delay the feeding of the delegates, and the Bishops agreed with me. But the host Bishop explained that all arrangements had been put in place to ensure that feeding would not be delayed. We gave him the benefit of the doubt, but I said, 'God will not let any of us die. We will be alive to attend this meeting, to see if there will be no delay in the feeding of the delegates as a result of the distance between the two venues.' I vividly remember Bishop Innocent Ordu looking at me and smiling.

As we gathered together to conclude our visit with prayer, one of the Bishops prayed, thanking God, and in closing, I said in prayer very casually, 'God, please take us to our various destinations safely. We have no reason to expect any accident on our way back. We have every reason to believe that You will lead us, Your servants, home safely. We have come to do Your work. Please lead us home safely, in Jesus's name.' Some Bishops and their wives smiled at that prayer, perhaps because it was so casual, as if I was discussing with my friend.

The trip home was smooth, and I called each of them at intervals to ensure they had no problem on the way back. Due to the traffic jam in Port Harcourt City, we arrived home at about eight thirty (8.30 p.m.). We had a programme in the city the following morning, Saturday, which was also a day of sanitation (in the Rivers State, the first Saturday of the month is set aside for general clean-up of Rivers State). Sir Ngozi and Dame Kate Abu had their daughter's wedding that Saturday, and we had to leave that night so as not to violate the sanitation order. Ngozi Abu was the accountant general of Rivers State, Nigeria, at that time. No one was allowed to move freely until after ten (10 a.m.) on such a day, and usually, after 10 a.m., the roads would be locked up in heavy traffic, because almost everyone with a vehicle would be on the road. Sometimes it would take three to four hours to get to one's destination. In order to avoid being late to the programme, we agreed to leave for the city that night so that people at the programme would not have to wait for us for hours. My wife, Beatrice, was not comfortable with this arrangement. She protested lightly, but I insisted.

She and I left our house at about 10.30–11 p.m. The route we followed was the usual road we took whenever there was a traffic jam; we could travel that road back home at about 2 a.m. We had not travelled up to three kilometres when we got to a very bad spot where all vehicles had to slow down because of the potholes on the road. In the course of our journey, we came to the point where we were halted by three young men who were there waiting and who emerged from a car in front of us. They accosted the driver of our vehicle, Eric. They were hitting the glass on the driver's side, but the driver refused to open. Innocently, I directed him to open the window. My wife thought they were a vigilante group who sometimes used to police the town to ward off criminal elements.

My wife told them in the local dialect that we were Eleme people. But it seemed as if that did not make any sense to them. The driver told them, 'This is the Archbishop.' They still insisted he should come down. Beatrice emphatically said, 'This is the Archbishop.' They still insisted the driver should come down. They dragged him down, and one of the young men took the driver's seat. The other moved in from outside and sat down at the right side of the driver's seat (Nigeria uses LHD). The third person opened my side of the car and sat by my side.

I was in my full regalia, just as I dressed in Yenagoa, with my pectoral cross, my episcopal ring, my cassock, and my skullcap. It was not an error. It was deliberate. They drove off while Beatrice was praying aloud; they asked her to keep quiet. I knew there was a problem. They drove very fast and, after a few minutes, veered off the highway into a bushy rough road. We had not been there before. After driving us far along that road, they stopped the vehicle. It was very dark. They searched my briefcase and Beatrice's handbag and took all the money. I then thought they were armed robbers. I saw a gun on one of them. I thought that after searching us and robbing us, they would let us go.

They asked us to come down from the car. It had rained that day; the ground was slippery, and there were puddles of water. The car was left open, with the key in the ignition, as they marched us into the bush. After about a kilometre walk, Beatrice fell down because the ground was slippery.

I had to lift her up. I jacked her up by her left, and one of them jacked her up by her right; we supported her as we moved. They were in such a hurry and said again, 'Madam, the journey is still long' After about a two-kilometre walk, we were taken into a 'transit camp', and all of us sat on the floor. There was no light except the light from their mobile phones. My wife's phone rang. It was a call from my daughter, Jane. They took the phone from my wife and responded. 'We have kidnapped your papa and mama,' they told her bluntly. At this point, it became very clear that we had been kidnapped. Beatrice was still praying aloud, to their discomfort. They did not want any noise that would lead to their detection. 'We will shoot you now if you don't keep quiet.' Sitting beside her, I tapped her legs to make her keep quiet or pray without a voice. Now it may interest you to know the mild drama that ensued between us and the hoodlums:

I: Please, can you let me say something?

Kidnappers: Okay.

I: Please let my wife go.

Beatrice: I will not leave you here alone.

I: Please let her go. D, please, you have to go. (I call my wife D most of the time.)

Kidnappers: Madam, do you hear what your husband said?

Beatrice: Please I will not go. I will not leave my husband here. I will go with him wherever you take him to.

I (to Beatrice in my local dialect): You will have to go, please.

Kidnappers: Oga (Master), we will let you go.

I: No, my wife should go so that she will negotiate for my release.

They conferred amongst themselves. God touched their hearts.

Kidnappers: Madam, you will go.

Beatrice protested, but I was glad they did let her go. We all left the bush and went back to the road. 'Madam, you will go straight. You will see your car. Your car is facing left. Don't go that way. Go the opposite way—to the road.' The darkness around could be felt. I was afraid that she would walk about two kilometres alone in the bush.

'Please, can one of you escort her to the car with a gun?' 'No, let her go,' they replied. I was more afraid. How could she make it back to the car? I pondered the consequences: if another group would kidnap her on the road or if she would encounter a wild beast. I forgot my ordeal and started praying for her. They removed the SIM card from her mobile phone and took her phone from her. They gave her another phone with a light. She was already wearied and worn out, having been on the road to and from Yenagoa and having trekked about two kilometres—the trauma, the emotional state. I had no choice but to pray for her. 'Madam, don't look back. Go. *Oga* [Master], the journey is long,' the hoodlums thundered at us.

Three of them and I walked another three or four kilometres into the bush in the dark. Sometimes we crossed some roads or footpaths. I was not allowed to look up, but I saw some cables. I was not sure whether those cables were telephone lines or electricity lines, but there were very high poles supporting them. I was really worn out and wearied, and I remember praying these words in silence:

> Our Father, which art in heaven, hallowed be Thy Name. Thy kingdom come. Thy will be done on earth, as it is in heaven. Give us this day our daily bread. And forgive us our debts, as we forgive our debtors. And lead us not into temptation, but deliver us from evil: for Thine is the kingdom, and the power and the glory, forever. Amen.

> The Lord is my shepherd; I shall not want. He maketh me to lie down in green pastures: He leadeth me beside the still waters. He restoreth my soul: He leadeth me in the paths of righteousness for His name's sake. Yea, though I walk through the valley of the shadow of death, I will fear no evil: for thou art with me; thy rod and thy staff they comfort me. Thou preparest a table before me in the presence of mine enemies: thou

anointest my head with oil; my cup runneth over.
Surely goodness and mercy shall follow me all the
days of my life: and I will dwell in the house of
the Lord forever.

I lost count of how many times I repeated these two prayers. Yet my
wife's situation became a problem to me. Had she arrived safely?
What had happened to her? What trauma was she going through?
Several questions crossed my mind, but I resigned all to God.
Then we got to our destination—a small open space supported by
about six poles. There were benches, and I was asked to sit down
on one of them. That night, I slept on that bench, which was about
three-quarters of my height.

One of them woke me from sleep. I was given rice, fast food, and
what people now call 'pure water'—that water in a sachet. *'Oga,
you dey drink pure water?'* ('Master, do you drink sachet water?') 'I
have no choice,' I replied. I slept on that bench in the open shed
that night. It drizzled. I cannot remember when I last slept in an
open place. It was so dehumanising.

When I woke up, I heard people praying from afar. It was Friday
night, and many churches were in night vigil. I saw a storey
building (I can't remember how many storeys) but did not know
where I was. I asked one guard who was guarding me with a gun,
'What is the time now?' He replied, 'Where are you going now that
you want to know the time?' It might interest you to know about
this brief encounter I had with one of the kidnappers:

I: What church do you attend?

Answer: Roman Catholic.

I: Is this how you treat your priests? Can you treat your priests
this way?

Answer: (Silence.)

Very early in the morning, at about four o'clock, they woke me up, and for about a kilometre or so, we waded through the bushy, thick forest to a station. Perhaps they made us move away from that hut because it was getting to daylight and they did not want anyone to see us there.

At this second place, I slept on the bare floor with the rain falling. I was not allowed to see or face the kidnappers. Wherever we were, I was made to face the bush. It was only on the first day that my eyes were covered, though I was always made to face the bush to ensure that none of them could be identified by me. That day, Saturday, I told them I wanted to talk to my wife. I had been worried about her safety since I asked them to release her in the dead of the night. I was told, 'The person [boss] who has your phone is not here yet.' I always slept on bare ground, whether wet or dry.

One fateful day, I overheard a little boy pleading for his life. This boy was passing by close to where we were camped. 'Please don't shoot me' was the plea I heard several times. 'I am just passing by. Please don't kill me.' It seemed the boy was carrying something on his head. After about three days, the kidnapper who had been involved in this encounter related the story to his colleagues and said that if he had known, he would have seized (or confiscated) the garri (cassava powder) from that young boy.

Every time they heard any noise, they would move us away from that spot. The following morning (Sunday), we moved through the bush for about two kilometres. This took us about one hour. Sometimes we needed to crawl under the thicket of the bush. Helicopters flew overhead several times. Initially, I did not know they were searching for me, but when I looked up, the kidnappers warned me not to look up. Then it dawned on me that the helicopters were searching for my position. We must give credit to the police for that search, but I didn't think they would ever have seen me. I was told that the Governor of Rivers State, His Excellency Rt Hon. Chibuike Rotimi Amaechi, had arranged for two helicopters to go on a search for me. It was a forest, and the kidnappers always made sure that we were under thick leaves or trees or near an Indian bamboo cluster.

6

THE GOD OF ARCHBISHOP KATTEY

On the second day, I lay on the wet ground in the forest with my face away from the kidnappers, and then I prayed:

> God, this is the time for You to act. I remember that some three years ago, Barrister Isaac Kamalu's mother was kidnapped. (Barrister Kamalu was the Registrar of the Diocese of Niger Delta North.) When she was released from her kidnappers, she testified that she called on the God of Kattey, and the God of Kattey released her. Some three years ago, His Royal Highness, Sir Emperor Mkpe, was kidnapped. When he was released, he said the God of Archbishop Kattey set him free. Now, God, You are Almighty, all-powerful, and You have proved it by releasing these two persons

who were kidnapped. Now the Kattey whose
God released others is here. Do Your great
miracle and release him.

It seemed as if God did not answer that prayer. One thing everyone
must note is that God is not sentimental. He has His own plans and
strategy, and He would never succumb to sentimental prayers. He
is sovereign and takes His time to work out His plan and purpose.
It depended on Him, the sovereign Lord, to allow me to live or
die, to release me or not.

In Acts 12, King Herod killed James, the brother of John, and
went ahead to arrest Peter in order to please the Jews, who were
antagonistic of the new faith. But God decided to release Peter
miraculously. Why did He decide to release Peter, but He allowed
James, the brother of John, to be killed by the wicked king? The
hymn writer William Cowper seems to supply us the answer in the
last stanza of his hymn 'God Moves in a Mysterious Way':

> Blind unbelief is sure to err
> And scan His work in vain
> God is His own Interpreter
> And He will make it plain.

Why was it that John the Baptist, who was deliberately sent to
prepare the way for Christ, was allowed by God to be killed in a
most gruesome and shameful way? John the Baptist was beheaded
in prison, and his head, dripping with blood, was placed on a platter
and given to Herod. He handed it over to Herodias's daughter,
Salome, just because she did a good dance that impressed Herod,
who, in turn, made an 'open-cheque promise'.

A very unlikely person became the king of Israel—the son of an
adulterous woman who made the 'man after God's heart to sin',
though perhaps it was not her fault. Apostle Paul describes God as

'he who is blessed and only Potentate, the King of Kings and Lord of lords, who alone has immortality, dwelling in unapproachable light, whom no man has seen or can see, to whom be honour and everlasting power. Amen' (1 Timothy 6:15–16).

In his letter to the Roman believers, Paul wrote about the election and the irrevocability of the gift of God and His sovereignty, to a point that Uncle Paul was moved to exclaim:

> Oh the depth of the riches both of the wisdom and knowledge of God! How unsearchable are His judgments and His ways are past finding out! 'For who has known the mind of God, or who has become His counselor? Or who has first given to Him and it shall be repaid to Him' for of Him and through Him and to Him are all things, to whom be glory forever. Amen. (Romans 11:33–36)

The world belongs to God, and He has every right to do with it anything He wants. If He wanted me to be killed, that could have been the best for me. I am His child. He created me. I did not create myself. He saved me. I did not save myself. When I was in sin, He allowed Jesus Christ, His only Son, to die for my sins.

'I WILL SHOOT YOUR LEG': A DEAFENING THREAT

Within two days, I was taken to about four locations in the forest. On the Sunday following the Friday night of kidnap, I became very worried about the safety of my wife. I repeatedly told them I wanted to know about her welfare. My guards said their boss would arrange for that. The boss came much later on Sunday, for the first time. He gave me the number, and he called her (that was when I knew that it was the alternate mobile phone that was taken from her). I was very elated and at peace when I heard her voice. She asked, 'How are you?' 'I am fine,' I responded. This angered the boss. He shouted at me, 'I will shoot your legs now so that you will know that you are not fine!' (I did not know Beatrice heard this threat.) He intended to intimidate me so as to keep my wife panicking. He took the phone from me and spoke to my wife.

'Have you been to Brazil before?' the boss asked me. I answered no.

'Brazil TV is announcing your name. Imagine Amaechi saying we should release you. Oh, one hundred million naira [which is about seventy thousand dollars or about twenty-five thousand pounds]. Give me Jonathan's number,' he continued. 'I don't have his number.' 'What of Obasanjo?' 'I don't have his number. You know I lost my phone in the course of our journey on Friday night.' 'You mean you don't have their numbers *off head*?' (The only number I am sure I know 'off head' is my wife's phone number.)

He seemed frustrated. I was too. The boss warned, 'If your people involve the police, we will finish you before the police get us.' This was a constant threat. I had to make it a prayer point that the police or security agents should not attempt to rescue me. Even without his threat, it is a dangerous venture to attempt to rescue anyone who is kidnapped. From their behaviour, one would wonder if these kidnappers sucked the breast of their mothers. They seemed heartless, either due to their nature or the nature of their profession or the drugs they take. Those who kidnapped me smoked Indian hemp *per second per second*.

THE PRECIOUS BREAD

All the rains that fell during that period fell on me. I was drenched in my episcopal wears, and my underwear was not spared. They kept me very cold. It seemed my underwear was becoming an issue for me, because they participated in keeping me uncomfortable. After a time, I removed my singlet to ease my discomfort.

On one of the rainy days, I slept beside Indian bamboo, the den of reptiles, and was very cold; I was not allowed to snore. 'Master, if you reveal us by your snore, we shall shoot you first before they kill us.' That day, I was sleeping on wet floor. In fact, one day, it rained cats and dogs. My guards felt for me. I was lying in a pool of water. I had no choice. One of my guards woke me up and asked me to stand up. I did so but could not stand up for long; age was not on my side. Rather than collapse, I lay down again in the water on the ground but felt very cold.

The day I was sleeping beside the mini Indian bamboo forest, it was very dark and cold, and I was surrounded by armed guards. I had lost sense of time, but I think it was not anything earlier than the midnight hour. One of them took advantage of the fact that I was sleeping, and he went into the town to buy things. He woke me up. I thought we were to move again to another location. But rather, he handed over to me a big flat piece of sliced bread and a polythene bag tied at one end to prevent spillage. 'Oga, take your mouth, open the top, and drink it from there.' It was warm. It was tea with sliced bread. Oh! That was one of my happiest moments during my kidnap. I had needed something warm. I cherished that kindness. I thanked him and, in that thick darkness, consumed it religiously. The strangest thing about it was that the person who did me that kindness was the boy who told me he was a Muslim! I heard my captors sing church hymns and choruses. I heard one sing about Elijah, though now I cannot remember the words.

HUNTERS' DOGS (404)

One day, as I was lying down on bare ground as usual, I heard some noise about twenty-five yards away in the forest. Still lying down (as I was not allowed to sit down or stand up, except when we were about to change locations), I saw a huge dog (in some parts of Nigeria, dogs are referred to as '404', named after the Peugeot car). I also heard human voices. My guards, who were sitting down, saw them and were terrified. The people talking came close to me; if they had moved a little closer, they could have seen me.

As soon as they turned back, my guards ran away, leaving me behind and abandoning their rifle. Somehow I think they met their leader. After some minutes, they came back for me and also collected their rifle. What happened later on made me guess what may have happened. When they took me to their leader, he was visibly angry, and he threatened, 'If the man had escaped, I could have killed both of you. Foolish people. You left the man you are asked to watch and your gun.'

As we were leaving that place, before we got to their leader, my guards asked me what those people with the dog were saying. Of course, I didn't tell them. After my release, I was told that some hunters took the risk of trying to rescue me. For this, I am grateful to them. If they had come with police dogs, they could have discovered me. Police dogs are well-trained for such tasks.

At another time, I heard some people singing some trade union or revolutionary songs in the forest.

m:r:d:f:l:- f:m.r: d.

'All we are saying, release Kattey.'

The kidnappers came to me and said, 'Your people are singing that we should release you.'

I did not know the singing was for me. The archdeacon in charge of Eleme Archdeaconry (Ven. Israel Omosioni) later told me he organised some youths to move into the forest to search for me. A big risk! They even went as far as blocking the highway and demanding my release.

I tried not to write down certain things in this book for security reasons. But in all, may God's name be honoured and glorified that I am alive today.

7

THE BEGINNING
OF MY RELEASE

I n one of the enclaves, very close to a stream, one of the guards asked me if I could swim. He felt their captive could jump into the water and swim away. But swim to where? We arrived there from another enclave because the kidnappers had heard some noise close by. We travelled through the thickets of the forest for about forty-five minutes. We were there on Wednesday and Thursday. At about five o'clock in the evening, one of the guards told the other that he was going home to repair the kitchen roof of his mother. That surprised me. The kidnapper had a mother; he was twenty-two. 'On Friday, I will not be here. Let Oga-Master come and discharge this Oga,' he said.

Then he called the boss on the phone. 'Oga, come and release this man. He has suffered much: a man like this lying on the wet floor in the bush for days. Mosquitoes have been biting him. I am going away tomorrow.'

I did not really hear the answer of his boss, but the guard was really serious and seemed bitter. He never spoke to him like a boss. I thought he might be a relation of the boss who had wanted some job, and the boss had offered him the job of guarding me.

After an hour or two, it was almost dark. The boss arrived. They were still talking to the boss; he was angry at them. 'What did this man give you that you are now pleading his cause?' He was really very angry. He spoke to them with great anger. I did not want the boss to transfer the aggression to me. I was sitting on the floor of the forest now, near the stream or river. He came to where I sat facing the bush. He kicked me and said, 'Whether you are a pope or whoever you are, we have kidnapped you, and we can kidnap anyone.'

What I had planned to do was get the boss to sit down, and talk with him and tell him to quit this 'job', and if possible, I could connect him to a real job. But when he talked about kidnapping a pope, I felt he was deranged.

'This night, I will be here with you.' I thought that he was going to release me that night because of the passionate pleas of the 'security guards'. At a certain time past midnight, we moved from that spot to another spot, crossing a pipeline road and farms. I slept that night with about eight of them surrounding me. I was hoping I would be released. I woke up at about 5 a.m. and asked, 'When will I be released?' There was no answer.

At about 7 a.m., the boss and five others left, leaving me with three guards. I noted that one of them was one of the three who did the actual kidnap. We stayed throughout Friday. The only serious event was the one-time food that we were given daily. The next day, Saturday, was also uneventful and boring. We did not move from place to place like other previous days. In the afternoon, one of the guards phoned the boss to ask him to send them food. This phoning was becoming more constant and aggressive from the guards' end; they felt we had all been abandoned, without food. I did not hear the response of the boss, but the guards were very bitter that the boss never cared to send them food. By evening, the situation remained unchanged, but as it was getting dark, we moved away through the forest for about forty-five minutes. We met a guard bringing food to the them and making their squirrel noise (by which they identified themselves), and they moved towards one another. It was dark, and one of them said, '*Oga, sit down. Make we eat*' ('Master, sit down, and let us eat').

As I sat down, they discovered we were very close to a track road in the forest. I was asked to move further from the track road into the bush. Then one of them said, '*I go leave this Oga. Make him go*' ('I will set this master free'). I heard him, but I thought they planned to shoot me. He said it again, but one of them was on the phone. The one on the phone said, '*Wait o, make I phone first.*' But the call was not going through, and he seemed to be angry that the call was not going through!

The man who said he was going to release me then said, 'Oga, take your wife's SIM card.' It was then I knew that the SIM card they used in calling was my wife's. In less than five minutes, he said, 'Take this two hundred naira [₦200]. Hold.' I was confused. What would I do with two hundred naira? (Two hundred naira is equivalent to a little above one dollar and a little below one pound.)

It was dark. He told me to use the two hundred naira for *Okada* (*Okada* is the Nigerian name for a motorcycle, which is used for transportation in some parts of Nigeria). At this point, the other two kidnappers told the third guard to take me to a convenient place. There, I prayed for forgiveness for them and advised them not to kidnap anyone again; otherwise, they would be caught. One of the guards carried a gaun, and I was asked to follow him. I still thought he was going to terminate my life that night. We went through the forest for about one hour, now all through track road. We did not make our way through the thicket of the forest again.

After precisely twenty minutes, we met the other guard again. They called to each other, and we continued our journey until we got to a certain point. My kidnapper said, "Oga, cross that road. You will see a tanker. Don't go right, go left. Find *okada*. Use the money I gave you. Enter *okada* and go.'

As I crossed the road, I saw light from a vehicle showing petrol tankers parked along the road. I trekked for less than five minutes, wrapping my cassock round myself to avoid being identified. An *okada* rider drove me to a point. Then another *okada* rider took me to my residence. I do not know if the *okada* rider knew who I was, because not only was it dark but also no one was expecting me at that time of the day.

8

DAILY COMMUNION WITH GOD

S omeone may ask, 'What were you doing for all those days and nights? Was it not very boring to be in the bush with strange people for those nine days?'

I am not sure it was boring, but it was very uncomfortable. I still had my *quiet time* (personal morning devotion), though it was in my heart. It gave me more time to pray. I worshipped God—the Father, the Son, the Holy Spirit. When I was not in captivity, most times I used to praise and worship God the Father on one day, God the Son another day, and God the Holy Spirit the next day. But when in captivity, I had enough time to worship the Holy Blessed Trinity in a day. I will reproduce the type of worship I did; I may not have used all the words, but I really did worship the Triune God.

WORSHIPPING AND PRAISING GOD THE FATHER
(i)

Almighty and everlasting God, Eternal King of Ages, King of kings and Lord of all lords, Alpha and Omega, the Beginning and the End, the First and the Last, the Holy One of Israel, the Most High God, Omnipotent, Omnipresent, Omniscience, Omnirighteous, Creator of the entire universe, Sustainer, Supreme Authority, El Shaddai, Adonai, Elohim, the Ruler of the whole universe.

You know far into the future, far into the past. The entire history of the universe is like a page before You, sovereign Lord.

Before ever You created the world, You had planned that Your Son Jesus Christ would be the Redeemer of the world. When Adam and Eve disobeyed You, You immediately proclaimed the *Protoevangelium*—that Christ Jesus would come to redeem mankind. Lord, thank You for Your foreknowledge and plan for salvation. You said, 'The seed of this woman shall bruise the head of the serpent.' You rejected Cain and his sacrifice. You accepted Abel and his sacrifice. Cain secretly killed Abel, but with You being omnipresent and omniscient, nothing could be hidden from You. You punished Cain. You heard the blood of Abel crying for vengeance on Cain. Praise be to You.

You translated Enoch to heaven because he walked with You. Lord, no man can satisfy You except by Your grace.

You pulled down the Tower of Babel when men conspired against You. You scattered them and gave them different languages. Father, You gave them different languages. People of all languages pray to You. You hear them all. Praise be to You.

You destroyed the world by means of a flood. You saved Noah and his family. You are omnirighteous. You never punish the righteous together with the wicked.

You asked Abraham to leave his land for a land he did not know. Abraham gave away his wife for fear of being killed. But You, Almighty, merciful God, quickly intervened. You sent plagues to the Pharaoh for him to return Abraham's wife. You warned King Abimelech, king of Gerar, 'Behold, you are a dead man because you have taken my servant's wife.' Lord, You take care of and guard the possessions of Your children. Praise be to Your holy name.

When Lot chose a better place to dwell in, You still blessed Abraham with much more than Lot. You also empowered him to defeat six powerful kings in order to rescue Lot from their hands.

You promised Abraham that the number of his children would be as great as the number of stars in the sky and the number of sand on the seashore. At this time, he was about one hundred years old and his wife, Sarah, about ninety-nine years old. You promised him, first of all, Isaac, whom You gave to the barren old Sarah at the appointed time.

You told Abraham to sacrifice by killing his only child, the child he had in his old age. He was going to do it, but You immediately stopped him and gave him a ram. You always wish the best for Your people.

You condescended that Abraham could intercede for Sodom and Gomorrah to be spared by You. You could not even find ten righteous men in those cities.

You had no alternative than to destroy the city, but You saved Lot and his people. Lot's wife turned into a pillar of salt for disobeying Your command not to look back.

Our Lord and our God, You chose a beautiful bride for Isaac. Rebecca was barren, but You opened her womb. She delivered Esau and Jacob. You said, 'Esau I have hated, but Jacob I have loved.' In accordance with Your Word, You made Esau sell his birthright to Jacob. You made it impossible for Esau to kill Jacob, his brother.

You revealed Yourself to Jacob. Firstly, You made him see Your holy angels ascending and descending a ladder from heaven. You changed his name from Jacob to Israel. You warned his cousin Laban not to say any word of scolding or anger to Jacob.

You gave Jacob Leah and Rachael. Rachael was barren. You opened her womb to deliver Joseph and Benjamin. You spoke to Joseph in a dream and said that all his brothers should bow before him. In innocence, he told the dream to his brothers. In hatred, his brothers were determined to frustrate Your promise to him. They planned to kill him, but immediately, in order to accomplish Your purpose, You gave them another suggestion. Joseph was sold to some slave dealers You provided—Ishmaelites—and they took Joseph to Egypt and sold him to Potiphar, the captain of the king's guard.

You blessed Potiphar because of Joseph, for You were with Joseph; the whole household of Potiphar was handed over to Joseph as overseer. Potiphar's wife lusted after Joseph, but You made it impossible for Joseph to commit sin with her. Maliciously, he was sent to jail. Lord, You made him overcome that temptation, and we depend on You to enable us to overcome similar temptations.

In prison, Joseph was made the overseer because You were with him. You sent to prison the king's chief butler and chief baker. You gave them dreams—the chief baker was hanged, and the chief butler was released and restored after three days. In spite of the plea of Your servant Joseph, the chief butler forgot all about him, but You never forget about Joseph. At the appointed time, You made the pharaoh have a dream, and You made sure no one, not even his magicians and enchanters, could interpret it. You made the pharaoh send for Joseph. You revealed the interpretation of the dream to Joseph. You made the pharaoh promote and lift him out of jail to become the Governor of Egypt. Soon after, You made Joseph's brothers bow down to him, in order that Your Word and promise be fulfilled. Lord, may You receive the praise and honour and glory forever and ever.

When a king arose that did not know Joseph, he ordered that all male children born to Hebrew women be killed as they are born. But You asked Your angels to be midwives for Hebrew women. They delivered without the aid of any visible being. You save Moses in the bush near the river. You made him escape death and trained him in the courts of the pharaoh. At the appointed time, You appeared to him in far Midian. You said, 'I have heard the cry of my people of Israel. I have seen the oppression which the Egyptians subject them to, and I have come to deliver them. My name is I-Am-Who-I-Am. I make You god to the pharaoh, and Aaron I have given you as your prophet.' You met Moses in a bush of Midian. There was fire in the bush, but the bush never got burnt.

You told Moses to drop the rod on his hand. It turned into a serpent. You asked him to pick it up by the tail. It turned back into a rod. You told Moses to put his hand into his shirt, and it turned leprous. You told him to put it back a second time, and his hand returned to normal. You told Moses, 'Go to the pharaoh. Tell him to let my people go.' The pharaoh refused. You sent him a plague of frogs, a plague of flies, a plague of locusts, and thick darkness. You sent the pharaoh thunder and hail, You sent boils, and finally, You sent Your angels to kill all the firstborn sons of Egypt and spared all the firstborn sons of Israel.

When You made Your people, Israel, leave Egypt, they left as victors, not as poor slaves. You led them with a pillar of cloud by day and a pillar of light by night.

When they got to the Red Sea, they were in trouble. The Red Sea was in front of them, mountains were on their sides, and the Egyptians' well-trained army of vengeance was behind and close to them. You caused darkness to separate the Egyptian army from the unarmed Israelites. Moses, Your servant, told them, 'Stand still, and you shall see the salvation of God.'

You truly did not put Your servant to shame. You opened the Red Sea, and the Israelites passed through dry land in the Red Sea. But as the Egyptians were passing through the Red Sea, You closed up the sea to swallow them. You fed Your people with manna, the food of angels, in the wilderness. You gave them water to drink from a rock. You took Your servant Moses to Mount Sinai, where You gave him the Ten Commandments for men. You proclaimed Yourself as 'the Lord! The Lord! A God merciful and gracious, slow to anger, and abounding in steadfast love and faithfulness. Keeping steadfast love thousands, forgiving iniquity and transgression and sin but who will by no means clear the guilty, visiting the iniquity of the fathers upon the children and the children's children, to the third and the fourth generation.' Lord, I believe You are what You say You are. Praise be to Your holy name.

Moses, Your servant, proclaimed You as 'the Rock, Your work is perfect. All Your ways are justice. God of faithfulness and without iniquity, just and right are Your ways.' Truly, Lord, Your work and ways are perfect. I agree with Moses.

(ii)

You, the eternal God, replaced Moses with Joshua; You told Joshua, 'This Book of the Law shall not depart from your mouth, but you shall meditate upon it day and night, that you may be careful to do all that is written in it; for then you shall make your way prosperous and then, you shall have good success.

'Be strong and of good courage; Be not frightened, neither be dismayed; For the Lord your God is with you wherever you go.'

Lord, You kept Your promise. You were with Your servant Joshua. You told him to run round Jericho once a day for six days and seven times on the seventh day. You sent Your angels to push down the historic great walls of Jericho. You stopped the sun for about a day; there were two days in one day because of Your servant Joshua, until he won the war.

O Lord God of Gideon, with only 300 ill-equipped soldiers of Gideon, You defeated 135,000 well-armed soldiers of Midian. No one but Jehovah-Nissi could do that—300 men defeating 135,000 men. Lord, You are great. You are powerful. You are the Lord strong and mighty, the Lord mighty in battle. Hope of the hopeless, help of the helpless, comfort of the afflicted, wealth of the poor. You heard and answered the prayer of the poor woman Hannah. You moved into her heart. She did not utter a word. You gave her a child, Prophet Samuel, and later on, You opened her womb. She had five more children. Praise be to Your holy name.

'There is none beside Thee; there is no rock like our God.' You are God of the poor, King of the poor. Many kings cannot answer poor women, but You did, O Lord our God.

(iii)

You chose David from the bush to be king of Israel, the greatest position in the whole world. You left all his elder brothers, who were relaxing in their houses. You left all the big families and big, strong men. You decided to choose a poor boy, a shepherd who was not even present at the place of selection, to be king of Your people. King Saul, whom You demoted for disobedience, tried all means to kill the one You anointed. But mortal men cannot kill God's anointed in God's own world. Rather, You played King Saul into the hands of Your servant David on two occasions. David did King Saul no harm because of You. You delivered David from the hands of King Saul.

You empowered David to tear lions and bears to pieces with the physical hand. You made small boy David defeat giant Goliath of Gath and cut off his head. When Absalom rebelled against Your servant David, Ahithophel, the greatest counsellor in Israel, joined Absalom. This meant no hope for King David, but David trusted You and prayed, 'O Lord, I pray Thee, turn the counsel of Ahithophel into foolishness.'

You did it in a miraculous way. You made Absalom reject the good counsel of Ahithophel. Ahithophel went and committed suicide, and Absalom, David's rebellious son, was seen hanging on a tree. He was killed in the war.

Adonijah proclaimed himself king without Your approval. You removed him and made Solomon, the son of the adulterous Bathsheba, the king of Israel. Your ways are strange.

Who can understand Your ways, O Lord? You gave Solomon wisdom that he became the wisest man ever on earth. You alone choose. You are Your own counsellor.

Elijah cried out to You. You stopped the rains for three and a half years in Israel. He prayed again, and You sent rains back. He prayed, and You sent down fire from heaven to consume his sacrifice in the presence of all Israel. Elijah told the Zarephath woman, 'The jar of meal shall not be spent, and the crude of oil shall not fail until that day that the Lord sends rain upon the earth.' It happened as Your servant Elijah had said. Elijah prayed to You. You brought back to life the dead son of the kind Zarephath woman. You took Elijah to heaven without death. Elisha prayed that

You give him double portion of the power and the spirit You gave to Elijah. You did so.

Your servant Elisha, by Your power, helped a poor widow pay her debts by asking You to provide, miraculously, oil in her vessels. You gave a son to a barren woman, the Shunammite woman, by the word of the man of God, Elisha.

When this child died, through Your servant Elisha, You brought the child back to life. You made Your servant Elisha hear all the evil plans of the godless king of Syria against Your people, Israel. When the pagan king of Syria sent his troops to arrest Elisha, You blinded them at the prayer of Elisha. 'Those who are with us are more than those who are with them.' You proved this, for when You opened the eyes of Elisha's servant, he saw the mountain full of horses and chariots of fire with Your angels riding them.

You are Lord God of hosts. The king of Syria besieged the city of Samaria so that there was a great famine. Elisha told the king, 'By this time tomorrow, food will be surplus and cheaper than at normal time.' But the captain, the king's batman, said, 'Even if God opened the window of heaven for food to fall, could this thing be so?' Elisha, Your servant, then said, 'You will see the surplus food, but you will not eat any of it.'

That same night, the Lord sent His angels to make a loud noise. The Syrian soldiers said, 'Oh, the king of Israel has hired the kings of the Hittites and the Egyptians to fight us.' But it was Your army.

The Syrians fled and left all their food, property, and ammunitions. Food became surplus, as the man of God had said. The captain was asked to be at the gate to monitor the movement of the food. He died in a stampede, for he was trampled to death without tasting the food, according to the word of the man of God. Lord, You confirm the words of Your servants.

Hezekiah, Your servant whom You made king, prayed to You at the point of death. You gave him fifteen extra years to live. Life and death are in Your hands. Sennacherib, king of Assyria, boasted that he was going to bundle Jehovah and throw him into the fire as he did the false gods of Hamath, Arpad, Sepharvaim, Henna, and Ivvah. He forgot that You are the immortal invisible God of creation. At midnight, You sent Your angels to destroy 185,000 soldiers of Sennacherib at the prayer of King Hezekiah, Your servant. You made the sons of Sennacherib assassinate him for saying he was going to destroy Jehovah.

The Ammonites, the Amorites, and the people of Mount Seir conspired against the people of Judah. King Jehoshaphat cried out to You and raised praises to You. You made them fight against each other, and Judah went to clear the remnant. Lord, You have Your own ways. You make conspirators against Your people fight amongst themselves.

Esther was a slave. You made her queen of the land, the wife of King Ahasuerus. You alone promote and demote. Mordecai was a slave and a gateman. Haman the Wicked wanted to kill him because Your servant Mordecai refused to worship him as others did.

The night before the day Haman planned to hang Mordecai, You kept King Ahasuerus awake. You woke him, and for no reason, he started going through files and books of records at midnight.

You made him see where it was written that Mordecai, the slave and gateman, reported a plot to kill him. For Mordecai's reward, the king summoned Haman to ask him what good the king could to do honour a favourite. Haman, thinking it was him the king wanted to honour, told the king to set the person to ride on the king's favourite horse with the king's used robe as his apparel, and to proclaim round the city that the favourite was next to the king. The king said to wicked Haman, 'Go, do so to Mordecai.' Lord, You are great. You uplift people who are low.

Mordecai became the Prime Minister, next to King Ahasuerus by the power of God. Haman was hanged on the gallows which he himself had prepared to hang Mordecai.

Daniel was a slave. You made him Prime Minister of Babylon. Daniel was thrown into the lion's den because he refused to pray to the king; instead he prayed to You. Oh God, You delivered him from being eaten by hungry lions. You made lions befriend him.

Shadrach, Meshach, and Abednego were slaves. You made them chief prefects of Babylon. They were thrown into the fiery furnace. You delivered them by Your mighty power. You made them sing praise to You and dance in the fire. You made the fire cool their bodies. There is none like You. You humiliated Nebuchadnezzar. He refused to heed Your warning to stop being wicked.

You made him, great King Nebuchadnezzar of Babylon, become like a beast, eating the grass. You made him mad for seven years until he realised that You are Jehovah, the sovereign God who rules over the entire universe and gives the kingdom to whosoever You will.

You humiliated King Belshazzar. You warned him not to insult Your majesty because You allowed him to defeat Israel and destroy Your temple. He carried the vessels from Your sanctuary and drank wine with them.

With his lords, his wives, and his concubines, he praised the gods of gold and silver, bronze, iron, wood, and stone. He refused to heed the warning You gave through Your servant Daniel. You went as far as writing on the wall for him to read. He was stubborn. That very night, You caused his assassination, and You replaced him with Darius the Mede.

You are the same God who heard the prayer of Jonah in the belly of the fish. You rescued him. We hear of great men and women whom You blessed and lifted up above their colleagues, but these men and women later on turned against You and Your servants, proclaiming themselves gods to be worshipped. Lord, in Your eternal power, You humiliated them all.

King Herod threw Peter, Your servant, into jail, hoping to kill him the next day, but that same night, in answer to the prayer of Your people, Your angels went to jail and released him. The gates of iron were no obstacles to Your saving power. King Herod became so puffed up that he gladly accepted the praise and glory due to only God. You sent worms to eat him up in public. He died from this.

El Shaddai, Our All-Sufficient God
Eloheenu, the Lord My God
Jehovah Sabaoth, the Lord God of Hosts
Jehovah Tsidkenu, the Lord Our Righteousness
Elohim, Our Eternal Creator
El Gibbor, the Mighty God
El Olam, the Eternal God
Jehovah Rapha, the Lord Our Healer
Jehovah Ropheka, the Lord Our Healer
Adonai, the Sovereign Lord, Our Master and Owner
Eloheeka the Lord Your God
Mekaddishkem, the Lord Our Sanctifier
Jehovah Elyon, the Lord Most High
Jehovah Rohi, the Lord My Shepherd
Jehovah Jireh, the Lord Will Provide
Jehovah Hoseenu, the Lord Our Maker
Jehovah Nissi, the Lord Our Banner
Jehovah Shalom, the Lord Our Peace
Jehovah Shammah, the Lord Is Present
Eternal Father, You are gracious; You are wonderful and deserve honour and majesty. May

all the angels worship You. May the twenty-four elders and four living creatures worship and prostrate themselves before You. Receive power and blessings now and always, in Jesus's name, amen.

WORSHIPPING AND PRAISING GOD THE SON, JESUS CHRIST

Jesus Christ, the Son of the Living God
The Anointed One
The Alpha and the Omega
The Antidote against the Poison of Sin
The Author of Life
The Author of Eternal Salvation
Jesus the Greatest Architect
The Amen
The Arm of the Lord
Our Advocate
The Last Adam
The Attorney General of Sinners
The Beloved of the Father
The Bread of Life
The Bread of Life That Came Down from Heaven
The Blotter of Our Sins
The Begotten of the Father
The Brightness of God's Glory
The Beginning and the End
The Righteous Branch
The Royal Babe of Bethlehem
The Light Burden
The Beginning of the Creation of God
The Blessed and Only Potentate
The Burden Bearer
The Bishop of Our Souls

Barrister Jesus
Born of a Virgin's Womb
Born to Set People Free
The Chosen One of God
The Conqueror of Death
The Conqueror of All
The Consolation of Israel
The Care of the Aged
The Companion of the Rejected
The Chief Cornerstone
Jesus, the Holy Child
You Are the Captain of the Heavenly Host
The Chief Justice of the Universe
The Commander-in-Chief of God's Army
Consultant and Surgeon
Consolation of Martyrs
The Desire of the Nations
The Day Star from on High
The Strong Deliverer
Doctor Jesus
Immanuel, God with Us
The Eraser of Our Sins
Jesus, the Expert Engineer
The Firstborn of God
The Firstborn of All Creation
The Firstborn from the Dead
The Firstborn amongst Many Brethren
The First Name on the Lips of Children
The Friend of Children
The First and the Last
The Fortress
The Faithful and True Witness
The Governor of My Heart
The Greater than Aaron
The Greater than Jonah

The Greater than Moses
The Greater than Solomon
The Greater than Abraham
The Gate of Heaven
Jesus, the Giver of Life
Infinite Goodness
The True God and the True Man
The True Messiah
The Governor of the Universe
The Horn of My Salvation
The Head of the Church
The Head of All Spiritual Hierarchy
The Holy One of Israel
The Heir of All Things
The Holy Child of Bethlehem
The Divider of History
The Express Image of God
The Invincible
The Great I-Am-Who-I-Am
The Great Intercessor
Jesus of Galilee
Jesus the Conqueror
Jesus the Crown of Justice
Jesus of Nazareth
The Judge of the World
The Just One
The Righteous Judge
The Joy of Longing Hearts
The Joy of Angels
The King of Saints
The King of Kings and Lord of Lords
The King of the World
The King of Peace
The King of Heaven
The King of Glory

The Key of David
The Light of the World
The Light of Hope
The Last Name on the Lips of the Dying Faithful
The Loveliest of the Gift of God
The Lamb of God Who Takes Away the Sin of
the World
The Lion of the Tribe of Judah
Lover of Chastity
The Lord of Battles
The Lord of Glory
The Lord Mighty in Battle
The Lord of Might and Power
The Lord God of Hosts
Universal Monarch
Monarch of Monarchs
The Master of All Grand Masters
The Master of Apostles
The Man of Galilee
The Man of Calvary
The Name That Is Above Every Other Name
Our Mediator
The Overcomer
The Great Physician
The Great High Priest
Our High Priest of Endless Power
The Prophet of Prophets
Our Passover
Jesus, the World President
The Prince of Life
The Visa to Heaven
The Prize of Martyrs
The Universal Password
The Universal Justice of Peace (UJP)
Pastor Jesus

Jesus the Universal Vicar of the Church
The Resurrection and the Life
The Root of Jesse
The Redeemer
The Rose of Sharon
The Rabbi of Rabbis
The Rock of Ages
The Rock of Offence
The Son of Man
The Saviour of the World
David's Greater Son
Son of the Virgin Mary
The Bright and Morning Star
The Good Shepherd
The Chief Shepherd
The Great Shepherd of the Sheep
The Man of Sorrows, Acquainted with Grief
The Son of the Blessed
The Great Teacher
The Good Teacher
The Tower of David
The Tower of Ivory
The Unspeakable Gift
The Senior Advocate of the World (SAW)
The Lily of the Valleys
The True Vine, Your Father Is the Vine Dresser
The All-Time Winner
Jesus, Our Victory
Jesus, Our Champion
The Vicar of Vicars
Jesus, Our Landlord
The Way, the Truth, and the Life, No One Can
Come to the Father except Through You
The Wiser than Solomon
The Word of God

The Word of Life
The Word Incarnate
The Seed of the Woman
The Worship of the Angels
The Peer of Youths
The Easy Yoke
The A and the Z

Your name is the name that is above every other name. At the name of Jesus, every knee shall bow, whether in heaven, on earth, or underneath the earth.

You Are the Mighty God
Prince of Peace
Wonderful Counsellor
Everlasting Father
Field Marshal Jesus
Jesus, Prophet, Priest, and King
The Ruler of the King of the Earth
Jesus, Our Safeguard and Our Treasure
President Jesus, the President of the Universe
King of Patriarchs
Sun of Righteousness
Professor Jesus
Prime Minister Jesus, on Whose Shoulder Rests the Government and the Governance of the Whole World
He That Holds the Seven Stars in the Hand
He Who Was Dead and Yet Is Alive
He Who Has the Sharp Sword with Two Edges
He That Opens and That No Man Can Shut and That Shuts and That No Man Can Open
He Who Speaks Life into the Dead

He Who Has Eyes Like the Flame of Fire and
Feet Like Fine Brass
The Seat of Wisdom
The Reservoir of Knowledge
The Wisdom of the Foolish
The Strength of the Weak
The Joy of the Sad
The Peace of the Troubled
The Companion of the Lonely
The Solace of the Wretched
The Hope of Every Contrite Heart
The Fountain of Wisdom
The Cover of the Naked
The Boldness of the Frightened
The Boldness of the Coward
The Courage of the Coward
The Companion of Travellers
The Wealth of the Poor
The Rest of the Restless
The Defender of the Defenceless
The Defender of the Weak
The Mouth of the Dumb
The Ear of the Deaf
The Sight of the Blind
The Feet of the Lame
The Saviour of the Lost
The Rescuer of Those Going Astray
The Husband of Widows
The Father of the Fatherless
The Defender of Orphans
The Mother of the Motherless
You Made the Entire Universe, Things Visible
and Invisible
You Made the Angels and Lucifer Himself

You Made the Demon Spirits in the Water, on
Land, and in the Air
The World Made Flesh

In the beginning was the Word and the Word was
with God and the Word was God. The same was
in the beginning with God. All things were made
by Him, and without Him was not anything made
that was made. And the Word became flesh and
dwelt amongst us, and we beheld his glory as that
of the only begotten Son of God.

Jesus Most Absolutely Dependable
Jesus Most Admirable
Jesus Most Amiable
Jesus Most Bright
Jesus Most Faithful
Jesus Most Sweet
Jesus Most Compassionate
Jesus Most Blessed
Jesus Most Gentle
Jesus Most Noble
Jesus Most Gracious
Jesus Most Mighty
Jesus Most Innocent
Jesus Most Tender-Hearted
Jesus Most Holy
Jesus Most Affectionate
Jesus Most Kind-Hearted
Jesus Most Gracious
Jesus Most Loving
Jesus Most Priceless
Jesus Most Merciful
Jesus Most Meek
Jesus Most Clement

Jesus Most Chaste
Jesus Most Mild
Jesus Most Worthy
Jesus Most Excellent
Jesus Most Fearless
Jesus Most Victorious
Jesus Most Triumphant
Jesus Most Inviolate
Jesus Most Immaculate
Jesus Most Obedient
Jesus Most Marvellous
Jesus Most Perfect
Jesus Most Magnificent
Jesus Most Powerful
Jesus Most Pure
Jesus Most Reliable
Jesus Most Handsome
Jesus Most Sympathetic
Jesus Most Wonderful
Jesus Lover of Chastity
Jesus Our Banner
Jesus the Spotless
Jesus the Stainless
Jesus Most Venerable

You came down from heaven, lived a perfectly holy and stainless life. You said, 'As the Father has life in himself, so He has given the Son authority to have life in himself and to give life to whoever He will.'

You also gave us authority: 'Behold, I have given You authority [power] to tread on serpents and scorpions and over all the powers of the enemy, and nothing shall by any means hurt You.

'And these signs shall accompany all those who believe. In my name, they shall cast out demons. They shall speak in new tongues. They shall pick up serpents, and if they take any deadly thing, it shall not hurt them. They shall lay their hands on the sick, and the sick shall recover.'

Jesus, You healed the sick,
raised the dead,
opened the eyes of the blind,
made the dumb to speak,
made the deaf to hear, and
made the lame to walk.
Oh! Strength of Israel.

You were betrayed and, according to the scripture, mocked, tortured, and spat on. You were crucified on the cross of Calvary, where You shed Your precious blood. 'Surely, He had borne our sins and carried our sorrows. Yet we esteemed Him stricken and smitten of God and afflicted, for He was wounded for our transgression and bruised for our iniquities. And upon Him was the Chastisement that made us whole and by His Stripes, we are Healed.'

Thank You, Lord Jesus. You took our sins on Yourself. You were crucified. You died and were buried. On the third day, You rose again from the dead. You said, 'Behold, I have in my possession the keys of death and Hades.' After Your resurrection, You ascended into heaven, where You sit at God's right hand, interceding for us from Your throne.

You sent down the promise of the Father, the Holy Ghost. You are the Judge. For the Father has left all judgement to You, You will come, therefore, to judge the living and the dead. No one was worthy to open the seal and read its contents except You, oh Lord Jesus. You are coeternal, coequal, consubstantial with the Father and with the Holy Spirit.

You are the second person in the Blessed Trinity. May endless adoration, hallelujah, authority, blessings, dominion and glory, honour and majesty, might and power, praise and thanksgiving, wisdom and worship be ascribed to You both now and evermore. Amen.

WORSHIPPING AND PRAISING
GOD THE HOLY SPIRIT

The Holy Spirit
The Spirit of the Living God
The Spirit of God
The Spirit of the Lord
The Spirit of the Lord God
The Spirit of Wisdom
The Spirit That Was on Moses
The Spirit of Understanding
The Spirit of Counsel and Might
The Spirit of Knowledge and the Fear of the Lord
The Spirit of Grace and Supplication
The Spirit of Liberty
The Spirit of Christ
The Spirit of Jesus
The Spirit of Adoption
The Spirit of Abundance
The Spirit of Conquest
The Spirit That Cleanses Hearts

The Spirit of Creation
The Spirit of Service
The Spirit of Compassion
The Spirit of Discernment
The Spirit of Beauty
The Spirit of Glory
The Spirit of Prophecy
The Spirit of Miracles
The Spirit of Resurrection
The Spirit of Him Who Raised Jesus
The Spirit of Holiness
The Spirit of Wisdom and Revelation
The Spirit of Praise
The Spirit of Spirits
The Spirit of Decency
The Spirit of Orderliness
The Spirit of Tenderness
The Spirit of Redemption
The Spirit of Truth
The Spirit of Transformation
The Spirit of Sanctification
The Spirit of Promotion
The Spirit of Perfection
The Spirit Divine
The Spirit of Regeneration
The Spirit of Purity
The Spirit of Power and Discipline
The Spirit of Plenitude
The Spirit of Renewal
The Spirit of Unity
The Spirit of Utility
The Spirit of Comfort
The One Who Helps Us Cry Abba, Father
The Chief Administrator of the Universe
The Lord of All

The Alongside Helper
The Author of All Good
The Angels' Armour
The Anointing
The Another Comforter
The Assurance of Our Salvation
The Banisher of Barrenness
The Breath of God
The Breath of Life
The Buffer of the Believer
The Calmer of Every Fear
The Channel Through Which Blessings Reach Us
The Checks and Balances of the Believer
The Comforter of Hearts That Faint
The Companion of the Forsaken
Our Best Companion
The Chairman, Appointment and Promotion Board
The Consuming Fire
The Counsellor
The Creator Spirit
The Creation's Whole Desire
The Controller, God's Telephone Device
Colaborer with Gospel Ministers
The Pillar of Cloud
The Devil's Antibiotic
The Director, School of Prayer
The Director of Church Worship
The Director General of the Church Militant
The Expert in Spiritual Warfare
The Divine Dove
God's Holy Dove
The Director of Missions and Evangelism
The Director of Life

The Director, School of Linguistics and Languages
The Director General of Deliverance Ministry
The Element of Christ's Baptism
Our Enemies' Enemy
The Chief Executive of the Godhead
The Desired of God's Sweet Electric Current
The Fear of Lucifer
He Who Fills the Whole World
The Finger of God
The Fire That Purges
The Fountain of Joy
The Fountain of Peace
The Sweet Fragrance of God
Our Best Friend
The Fullness of God's Love
The General Manager of the Body of Christ
The General Overseer of the Universal Church
The Giver of Life
The Unfailing Guide of the Believer
The Faithful Guide
Best Gift of God
Celestial Flame
Our Guide and Guard
Gracious Spirit, in Charge of Church Growth
Great Spirit, in Charge of Church Planting
The Wanderer's Guide
The Best Gynaecologist
The Glowing Spirit
The Hater of Sin
The Help of All That Cry for Help
The Helper of the Redeemed
Heavenly Dove
The Hope of All Comfort
The Highest Spirit

Your Imperial and Sovereign Majesty
The Information Minister of the Godhead
The Inmate of Our Being
The Inspirer of the Word of God
The Interpreter of the Word of God
Our Great Intercessor
The Divine Instructor
The Inheritance of the Saints
The King of Invisible Powers
The Living Fire
The Interpreter of Sighs and Groans
Love Divine
Fire of Love
The Source of Life
The Eternal Fount of Love
The Light That Reveals
The Living Spring
The Pillar of Light
The Clear Leader
The Minister's Boss
Measureless Might
The Great Mover of Hearts
The Great Miracle Worker
The Fertilising Power
The Path of Life
The Glorious Power of the Trinity
The Publicity Secretary of the Eternal Godhead
The PRO of the Blessed Trinity
The Promise of the Father
The Purifying Fire
The Purest Spirit
Divine Presence
God's Perfume
The Sweet Unction
Our Senior Prayer Partner

The Paraclete
The Power from on High
The Physician Most Reliable
Professor of All Knowledge and Wisdom
The Provost of the Holy Trinity
The Power of the Highest
The Minister's Partner
The Preacher's Power
The Rushing Mighty Wind
The Ray of Heavenly Light
Refining Fire
The Reminder of Christ's Teaching
Our Resource Person
The Restrainer of the Man of Sin
The Registrar, Court of Heaven
The Sacrificial Flame
The Giver of Spiritual Gifts
The Source of Living Water
The Source of True Prophecy
The Splendour of All Aid
Our Shield and Defender
The Saint's Reward
Our Stronghold and Fortress
The Superintendent of the Prophets
The Source of Consolation
The Sweet Influence
The Sanctifier
The Softener of Stubborn Hearts
Our Unfailing Partner in Suffering
The Seal of God on the Believer
Our Security
The Shekinah Glory
The Sustainer of the Church
The Greatest Surgeon
The Most Sensitive Sin Meter

The Honourable Speaker for the Trinity
The Silent Power of God
The Strength of Our Heart
Divine Shock Absorber
The Teacher of Teachers
The Terror of Satan
The Third Person in the Glorious Trinity
Our Treasure Store
The Heavenly Unction
The Ever-Victorious Spirit
The Voice of the Almighty
The Gentle Voice
The Wind of God
The Wisest and Most Just
The Divine Wine
The Heavenly Witness, Chief Evangelist
God's Last Witness to Man

Jesus said, 'When You come, You will teach us all things and bring to our remembrance all the things He taught us.' You convict the world of sin, righteousness, and judgement.

Jesus said, 'If anyone speaks against the Father or the Son, the person will be forgiven. But anyone who speaks against the Holy Spirit, He can never be forgiven in this age nor in the age to come.'

You break every yoke.
You break bars of iron to pieces.
You open brass and iron gates.
You level all mountains.
You fill up every valley.
You dry up oceans.
You make rivers flow in the desert.

The Inspector General of God's Armed Forces.
The Supreme Commander of God's Armed Forces.
The Field Marshall of the Heavenly Hosts
The Field Commander of the Heavenly Army
The Chief of Staff in Charge of Administration
The Incomprehensible
Sovereign
Almighty
Omnipotent
Omniscient
Omnipresent
Eternal
Uncreated
Not Begotten
Proceeding from the Father and from the Son
Coequal
Coeternal
Cosubstantial with the Father and the Son.
May honour and praise, glory and majesty, power
and might be ascribed to You forever and ever.
Amen.

9

EARLY MORNING PRAYERS

As my custom was in my normal daily life, I used to sing some introit before I began my morning prayers.

> Holy, Holy, Holy, Lord God Almighty,
> Early in the morning our song shall rise to Thee
> Holy, Holy, Holy, merciful and mighty
> God in Three Persons, Blessed Trinity
> Holy, Holy, Holy all the saints adore Thee
> Casting down their golden crowns around the glassy sea
> Cherubim and Seraphim, falling down before Thee;
> Which wert and art and evermore shall be.

Then I will sing the refrain of the hymn 'Great Is Thy Faithfulness, Oh Lord My God'.

> Great is Thy faithfulness, Great is Thy faithfulness,
> Morning by Morning new mercies I see

All I have needed Thy hand hath provided
Great is Thy faithfulness, God unto me

In my daily family morning prayers, whenever I was asked to lead,
I started with these lyrics:

In the morning, early in the morning
In the morning I will rise and praise the Lord.
Good morning Jesus good morning Lord
I know You came from heaven above
The Holy Spirit is on the throne
We greet Jesus, good morning Lord.
I will gate His Gates with thanksgiving in my heart
I will enter His Court with praise
I will say 'This is the day that the Lord has made
I will rejoice for He has made me glad'
He has made me glad, I am so glad
I will rejoice for He has made me glad (2×)

THE LORD'S PRAYER

It is difficult to tell how many times I said the Lord's Prayer.

Our Father which art in heaven, Hallowed be
thy name. Thy kingdom come. Thy will be done
in earth, as it is in heaven. Give us this day our
daily bread. And forgive us our sin, as we forgive
those who sin against us. And lead us not into
temptation, but deliver us from evil: For thine is
the kingdom, and the power, and the glory, forever
and ever. Amen.

I said it as often as I was able to. If I did not pray it the way it is
usually prayed, I would use my own words in what I call the Lord's
Prayer Expanded, as below:

Our Father, almighty, omnipotent, omnipresent, omniscient, greater than all other fathers, I am Your child, a child You sought for while I went astray. Even now, I go astray often, but Lord, I still acknowledge You as my Father. *You are in heaven*, You are in me, You are on earth, You are everywhere. Truly, You dwell and reside in heaven. You use the earth as Your footstool. I am glad that poor, unworthy me, You use me as Your footstool. *Hallowed be Your name*. Praise be to Your name, the name above all names. But, Father, has any man ever known Your name? Father, man can only know Your titles—El Shaddai, Adonai, Elohim, Jehovah Jireh. Glory be to Your name, the 'I am who I am', the Lord God of hosts. *Thy kingdom come*. I pray, Lord, thy kingdom come. Help me hasten this by proclaiming Your Word. The world is rotten, filled with wars, lust, crime, oppression, confusion, and injustice, but Your kingdom is perfect in every sense of it.

Thy will be done in earth as it is in heaven. Father, thy will be done in my life. Lead me by thine own hand. Be thou my guide, my strength, my wisdom, and my all. Thy will shall be done on earth, only when Your kingdom has been established on earth just as it is done in heaven.

Give us this day our daily bread. Lord, You know that without You, I cannot live. The food I eat, the clothes I wear—all are bestowed by thee. Never let me starve, my Lord. Never let Your poor child starve. Though I am poor, I have a rich Father—'for the earth is the Lord's and the fullness thereof'. *Forgive us our trespasses*—they are numerous. There are those I know; there are many I do not know. Father, would You not forgive Your child the sins of his hands, sins of thought, deed, and word? If You do not forgive, who else can? Father, for this reason, You sent Your only begotten Son into this world to die for my sins. Use the precious blood of Your Son, Jesus, to cleanse me of all sins, hidden or exposed. If I say I have no sin, I am only deceiving myself. I have no excuse for any of my sins. I only ask You for forgiveness. I pray that You remember them no more, according to Your promises.

Truly, just as I offend You often, so many offend me too. I find it very difficult to forgive them, but I know by Your grace I will. I fear to say this, but, Father, I say it with boldness because I trust Your enabling. *Forgive us our trespasses, as we forgive them that trespass against us.*

Father, there are those who offend me, and I do not *know*. Please, I forgive them just as You forgive me the sins I do not know about.

Daddy, *please lead me not into temptation.* The world, the flesh, and the devil are around the path I tread. If I am tempted to sin, please, Lord, keep watch over me. Principalities and powers seek the slightest opportunity to attack me, so, Father, hold me by Your own hand.

But deliver us from all evil. Father, You have several times preserved me from death, from my mother's womb until now. Faithful Father, You keep me from danger every hour.

Please continue to guard me with Your ever watchful eye. Cover my defenceless head. Deliver me, Father, from the snare of the fowler and from the deadly pestilence, from known and unknown enemies, seen and unseen enemies.

My confidence, Lord, is that *the kingdom, the power, and the glory are all Yours.* You are sovereign, supreme, the Most High that rules the kingdom of men and gives it to whom You will. You are worthy to receive glory and honour and power, for You made all things visible and invisible; all things exist simply because You want it so. Father, may praise, glory, wisdom, thanks, honour, power, majesty, and strength belong to You and You alone. *Forever and ever. Amen.*

Psalm 23 was also my constant prayer. I lost count of how many times I prayed Psalm 23.

The Lord is my shepherd; I shall not want. He maketh me to lie down in green pastures: He leadeth me beside the still waters. He restoreth my soul: He leadeth me in the paths of righteousness for his name's sake. Yea, though I walk through the valley of the shadow of death, I will fear no evil: for Thou art with me; thy rod and thy staff they comfort me. Thou preparest a table before me in the presence of mine enemies: Thou anointest my head with oil; my cup runneth over. Surely goodness and mercy shall follow me all the days of my life: and I will dwell in the house of the Lord forever.

Psalm 23 is expanded below:

O Lord my God, You are my Shepherd. More than that, You are my Good Shepherd. I have no other person to trust to guide and guard me, except You. You know me very well and supply me all I need. I do not lack anything. You lead me to places You have already prepared for me. Everything is already made for me. You lead me from troublesome spots to quiet places. You refresh and restore my life. You give me new strength. You make me glad. You guide me in the right paths.

Your Spirit directs and guides me even when I am confused. You did this so that I might not disgrace Your name, Your precious name that is attached to my own name. My Lord, I will not be afraid even when I am at the jaws of death. When death wants to swallow me up, You are with me. You are in me. I will not fear. Your shepherd's rod protects me. Your rod protects me. Your shepherd's staff guides me.

Oh, how good is Your Word. You have poured Your untold and superabundant blessings on me where all my enemies can see me.

You have poured Your oil on me. You make me a king in my own small way, and no one can dethrone me because You have anointed me. You treat me as a special guest, although I do not deserve such honoured treatment. You have filled my cup to the brim. I am so sure and certain that Your goodness, love, and mercy shall be part of me all the days of my life.

I am glad that You will enable me to stay in Your house, amongst Your congregation on earth here, and when You call me home, I shall never depart from Your holy presence.

Thank You, Lord. Thank You, my God. Accept my thanks, which I offer through Jesus Christ our Lord. Amen.

One thing I know: I never prayed to be freed. I was always praising God. I was not even sure anyone was praying for me outside. But the Holy Spirit moved people all over the world to pray for me, and I thank God and all who prayed for my release.

10

SOLIDARITY CALLS AND VISITS

I t is pertinent to let the readers have an idea of the events that took place as soon as I was released.

The then Rivers State Commissioner of Police, Mr Joseph Mbu, an astute police officer, and his team paid us a visit in our residence. He offered to allocate to us some police escorts, which we declined. It must be noted that the then Governor of Rivers State, His Excellency, Chibuike Rotimi Amaechi, had told me he would arrange for me to have some police escorts as well, long before my kidnap. We did not think it was necessary. It is of note that Governor Amaechi appointed me as a member of the Truth and Reconciliation Committee of Rivers State, under the chairmanship of the fearless and disciplined retired judge, Justice Kayode Eso, as soon as he became Governor of Rivers State. This was when His Excellency, Nyesom Ezenwo Wike, was Governor Amaechi's chief of staff.

Governor Amaechi also called my wife during my kidnap to sympathise with her and assured her that efforts were being made to ensure my safe return. He also sent his Secretary to the State Government, Mr George Feyi, with a delegation, to visit my wife.

My wife told me the then Minister of Finance, the pride of all women, Mrs Ngozi Okonjo-Iweala, that great woman of international repute, called her on the phone to commiserate with her. Some months before then, her own mother had also been kidnapped.

The Primate of all Nigeria, His Grace, the Most Rev. Nicholas D. Okoh, with a team of Archbishops and Bishops, visited my wife and family twice. They were at Yenagoa, Diocese of Niger Delta West, for the Church of Nigeria Standing Committee meeting. They prayed for my release.

My former boss, His Grace, Most Rev. Peter J. Akinola, the immediate past Primate of all Nigeria, called to pray with my wife. The Rt Rev. Prof. Dapo Asaju, the then Dean of the Crowther Graduate Theological College, Abeokuta, a forefront theological college in Africa with sound biblical teachings, called to pray with my wife, assuring her prophetically that I would be released.

The Christian Association of Nigeria (CAN) of Rivers State paid a visit in their own capacity and also represented the national body. The Christian Council of Nigeria of Rivers State and the Muslim community in Rivers State were not left out, and we are thankful to all of them.

11

WHAT GOES ON IN THE MIND OF THE DYING?

It is pertinent to have an idea of what goes on in the mind of the dying, especially if they are conscious. I was not really afraid to die, but so many thoughts ran through my mind.

In my book *God Answers Prayer*, I guessed what was going through the mind of King Hezekiah when the Prophet Isaiah told him God's message that he should prepare himself and keep his house in order because his time on earth had expired.

What was on Hezekiah's mind as Isaiah left the room? Did he imagine himself dead and people around him wailing? Did he imagine the problem that would arise after his demise, since he had no son as heir to the throne? Did he imagine his coffin and its costliness? Did he imagine what good and evil things people would say about him? Did he imagine who would marry some of his wives?

For me, I thought first about my family, how they would fare after I died. How would my wife manage in my eternal absence? I started analysing all my children, one by one.

Someone would ask, 'Were you not thinking about the Diocese?' I did, but I didn't want to be overly concerned about the Diocese. After all, Christ is the Head of the Church. Apostle Paul, without mincing words, wrote to the believers in Ephesus, 'Therefore take heed to yourselves and to all the flock, among which the Holy Spirit has made you overseers, to shepherd the Church of God which He purchased with His own blood' (Acts 20:28). The Church belongs to God. I am simply an overseer, appointed by the Holy Spirit.

I was aware that when things like this happen, some people would be happy—pastors and laity. Some pastors would feel that my demise would be a good opportunity for them to be elected Bishop to replace me. I used to say that even if every city is made a diocese, not every pastor will be a Bishop.

Some of those I sanctioned or disciplined would rejoice that God was punishing me because I disciplined them for the offences they committed. Some would be praying for me, while some others would be praying *against* me. *This* is not unusual. Even some who would be secretly praying *against* me would openly lead prayer meetings, pretending to pray *for* my release.

One day, during my ordeal, I knew for sure that if I died in captivity, I would go to heaven. I had given my life to Jesus Christ in 1971 through the ministry of the Scripture Union, and by God's grace, I had not backslidden, even for one day. Salvation is by faith in Jesus Christ.

I remember when I was sick (that was the first time in my life I became sick to the point of being admitted to the hospital). It was so bad that my wife, Beatrice, had to request Rev. (now Venerable)

David Eguare, one of my trusted pastors, to fly to Abuja to stay with me. My wife later flew in. I was on admission. It was a hopeless case. Beatrice said I said to her, 'Thank you for all you have been to me, so dedicated, so faithful and caring. The children will bless you. Please take care of the children. God will help you.'

She said this put fear in her. She felt I told her those words because I was ready to die. I had given up hope to live. Dr Wakama was very helpful during this period. Dr Peter Akinola introduced me to Dr Wakama in the hospital. In my private hospital room, Beatrice was making phone calls with respect to my illness. I was facing the wall. I was conscious, so it wasn't a dream. I was standing for judgement. I saw the Father, the Son, and the Holy Spirit. I recognised them by the halo surrounding their heads. The others were seated with them in front of me, by my left, and by my right, but I don't think anyone was behind me. The devil suddenly appeared, standing by my left, accusing me of things I didn't hear, but I knew I was being accused. All I told him was that Jesus Christ, who was sitting in front of me, is my Saviour (I stretched my right hand towards Jesus when I said this) and that all questions, issues, and matters concerning me should be directed to him. The devil accused me a second and third time. I told him the same thing: 'Anything pertaining to me should be directed to Jesus Christ. He is my advocate.' Then I suddenly came back to myself, and I heard Beatrice making phone calls.

I didn't state my credentials in the church. That could have been fatal for me. I had a lot of credentials I could have presented to the devil.

'Do you not know that I am the Bishop of the Diocese of Niger Delta North, Church of Nigeria [Anglican Communion]? And that I am the Archbishop of the Province of Niger Delta, spanning over four states, viz. Cross River, Akwa Ibom, Rivers, and Bayelsa? And that I am covering thirteen dioceses?' And so on and so forth.

145

That could have spelt doom for me. But I referred the devil to the Victor; the Grand Master of all grand masters; He who was, who is, and who is to come; the Almighty; the One who conquered death after shedding His holy blood for my sins; the soon coming King; my personal Person; my Advocate; my Solicitor; my Attorney; my Defence Counsel; the Strong Deliverer—Jesus Christ, God's only begotten Son.

> And therefore, God also has highly exalted Him (Jesus) and given Him the Name which is above every name, that at the Name of Jesus, every knee should bow, of those in heaven, and of those on earth, and those under the earth, and that every tongue should confess that Jesus Christ is Lord, to the glory of God the Father. (Philippians 2:9–11)

Hear this from Apostle John:

> My little children, these things I write to you so that you may not sin. And if anyone sins, we have an Advocate with the Father, Jesus Christ, the righteous. And He is the propitiation for our sins, and not for ours only, but also for the whole world. (1 John 2:1–2)

Jesus Christ, surely, is my Advocate.

So during my kidnap, I was sure that, by God's grace, I would go to heaven, in the event that I died. I was not really afraid to die, but many thoughts ran through my mind concerning my family, as I stated earlier.

SOME PUBLICATIONS DURING AND AFTER THE KIDNAP

Nigerian archbishop is kidnapped

by Madeleine Davies

THE kidnapping of the Archbishop of Niger Delta Province in Nigeria, the Most Revd Ignatius Kattey (right), was a shock in an area where the threat to clerics is perceived to be minimal, an archdeacon from his diocese said this week.

The Ven. John Chukwuemeka Adubasim, of the diocese of Niger Delta North, was speaking on Tuesday, four days after the kidnapping took place near Port Harcourt, a city in the diocese. He is currently in the diocese of Guildford, which is linked to Nigeria, on a study visit, and was visiting a parish in the diocese when he received a call from Nigeria at 10.30 p.m. on Friday, informing him that both the Archbishop and his wife had been kidnapped.

"We were worried and started praying," he said. "About 12.35 a.m., I got a call that his wife, Beatrice, was released by the kidnappers; so I put a call to her to find out her situation. She was very worried and after some time of encouragement, she narrated how it had happened. They were on their way to Port Harcourt from their village and, as they were getting close to Port Harcourt, they were stopped by some armed men who pushed down the driver and took them some kilometres inside the bush. After some time they released her and asked her to go. Up to date, we have not heard from them; nobody has claimed responsibility for the kidnap; no calls have come in. That has made us very apprehensive."

Archbishop Kattey is Dean of the Church of Nigeria and thus its second most senior cleric. On Monday, the communications director of the province, Canon Taiwo Fabine, said: "We are praying that God in his infinite mercy will grant us, very quickly, the Dean's release from the hoodlums that took him."

On Monday, a police spokeswoman, Angela Agabe, told Reuters that police were hunting the kidnappers.

"We believe the Archbishop will be released soon going by the information available," she said.

The British Foreign Office reports that there is a "high threat" of kidnap throughout Nigeria, and insurers estimate that there are at least 1000 kidnappings every year. It is three years since the Bishop of Nghu, in south Nigeria, the Rt Revd Christian Ebosia, was kidnapped. He was released the next day.

On Tuesday, Archdeacon Adubasim said: "We have not had it this way before. I was [the Bishop's] chaplain for three-and-a-half years and we did not have any security issue on the Bishop, no attempt of any kind on him. That is why we are very much surprised at what is happening. In the recent times, Port Harcourt in particular has been very calm and peaceful. We are very shocked about this incident."

The militant Islamist group Boko Haram operates in the north of Nigeria, and the Archdeacon said that the south, which is overwhelmingly Christian, did not struggle with "intolerance".

He described the Archbishop, to whom he is "very close", as "a child of God . . . a peace-loving man . . That is why what is happening is very disheartening, because he embraces everybody as a family."

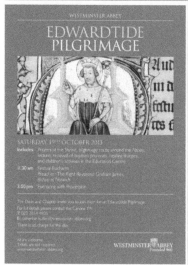
GHANA NEWS AGENCY

The Archdeacon reported that, since the enthronement of Bishop Kattey in 2000, about 158 churches had been planted in the diocese.

On Tuesday, the Bishop of Guildford, the Rt Revd Christopher Hill, who is scheduled to visit Nigeria in November, said: "We are deeply shocked. It brings it home to all of us when such a terrible thing is so close, and we have realised that through Archdeacon John being with us at the present time, and we are doing our best to support him, and of course are praying with a deep concern for Bishop Ignatius, Beatrice, his wife, and family, and we hope and pray for a good outcome."

UN discovers Ashraf bodies

A MAKESHIFT morgue at Camp Ashraf, home to hundreds of Iranian exiles in Iraq, was found by UN visitors to contain 52 bodies, all appearing to have suffered gunshot wounds, it was reported last week, writes *Madeleine Davies*.

The discovery follows an attack on 1 September. The UN Assistance Mission for Iraq visited the camp the next day.

"All the deceased appeared to have suffered gunshot wounds, the majority of them in the head and the upper body, and several with their hands tied," a statement said. The delegation also saw several damaged buildings, including one burnt, and was shown quantities of explosives."

The deputy special representative of the secretary-general of the UN, György Busztin, who led the visit, said: "I call on the Iraqi government to ensure that a thorough, impartial, and transparent investigation into this atrocious crime is conducted without delay, and that the results of the investigation are made public."

The director of the Association of Anglo-Iranian Women in the UK, Laila Jazayeri, said on the day of the attack that it had been perpetrated by Iraqi forces.

On Wednesday last week, the Archbishop of Wales, Dr Barry Morgan, said: "This vicious attack indicates that Maleki's government is either unable to or not committed to implementing and ensuring the safety, security and the well-being of a defenceless civilian population, who have been designated as 'Protected Persons' under the Geneva Convention and International Law."

Camp Ashraf is home to about 1500 Iranian exiles, many supporters of People's Mujahedin Organisation of Iran, which co-operated with supporters of Ayatollah Khomeni in toppling the Shah's regime in 1979.

"Oppressed": garment workers in Dhaka, Bangladesh, demand to be paid the minimum wage

Support for garment workers

by a staff reporter

A CHURCH-LED campaign will lobby for better working conditions and wages for Bangladeshi garment workers, in the wake of the more than 1000 deaths caused by a factory collapse earlier this year.

A global coalition of Churches launched the campaign in London on Thursday of last week, highlighting the fact that garment workers in Bangladesh are paid just ten pence an hour — only 14 per cent of the living wage in Bangladesh — and that 1800 workers have died in recent years in factory collapses and fires in the country.

The Rana Plaza factory collapse at Savar, Dhaka, in April this year, killed more than a thousand, and left thousands more injured. The factory made clothes for many British high-street stores.

The Moderator of the Church of Bangladesh, the Rt Revd Paul Sarker, said: "The Church of Bangladesh is passionate about the fight for social justice. Ongoing support from the wider community can help us to deliver real justice for this oppressed group of workers."

The coalition has produced resources to help consumers in the UK lobby for wage justice and better working conditions.

Steve Pearce, from the Methodist Church, said: "The distressing tragedy at Savar has given us the opportunity to take action and make a difference for garment workers in Bangladesh. As the story of the inexcusable loss of life at Rana Plaza fades from our media, I hope people will use these resources to make sure it doesn't fade from our memory before we have done our best to create irresistible pressure for change."

There are about four million workers in the clothing industry in Bangladesh, producing about 80 per cent of the country's export earnings.

The alliance of Churches working alongside the Church of Bangladesh includes the Church of Scotland, the Anglican Alliance, the diocese of Llandaff (Church in Wales), the Church Mission Society, the Methodist Church in Britain, Us (formerly USPG), and the Presbyterian Church of the Netherlands.

Archbishop Ignatius Kattey: Nigeria police seek kidnappers

🕐 9 September 2013   f 💬 🐦 ✉ < Share

Police in Nigeria are looking for the armed men who kidnapped the country's second most senior Anglican archbishop, Ignatius Kattey.

He was seized late on Friday, along with his wife Beatrice, near their residence in the southern city of Port Harcourt.

Ignatius Kattey is the head of the Anglican church in the restive Niger Delta

Mrs Kattey was released unharmed a few hours later, the church says.

Kidnapping for ransom has become common in the oil-rich Niger Delta region around Port Harcourt in recent years.

Last year the mother of Finance Minister Ngozi Okonjo-Iweala was abducted and held for five days.

No group has said it was behind the kidnapping of Archbishop Kattey, the head of the Anglican Church in the predominantly Christian Niger Delta.

Numerous armed gangs operate in the area following years of violent protests against the oil industry.

Share this story About sharing

Archbishop Kattey freed

THE Archbishop of Niger Delta Province in Nigeria, the Most Revd Ignatius Kattey, was freed on Saturday, more than a week after he was kidnapped by armed men (News, 13 September), *writes Madeleine Davies.*

He was released in a stable condition on Saturday evening without the payment of a ransom, police said. The kidnapping took place on Friday 6 September near the Archbishop's residence in the southern city of Port Harcourt.

Last week, Archdeacon John Chukwuemeka Adubasim, of the diocese of Niger Delta North, described how the kidnapping had been a shock in an area where the threat to clerics is perceived to be minimal.

On Tuesday, Archdeacon Adubasim said that a news conference in Nigeria had heard that the kidnappers had given the Archbishop money to return home. The Archbishop had said that he forgave them, and "handed them over to God".

On Sunday, the Archbishop of Canterbury gave thanks for Archbishop Kattey's safe return.

Chaplains visit site of killings

by a staff reporter

CHAPLAINS rushed to comfort the injured and grieving at the Washington Navy Yard, where 12 people were killed by a gunman this week.

A former US Navy serviceman, Aaron Alexis, died after a gun-battle with police at the Navy Yard on Monday morning. Reports suggest that he had mental-health problems, and was known to police for two previous gun-related incidents.

Naval chaplains on the base and others from bases near by, were brought in to assist those affected by the incident. Washington Cathedral offered prayers throughout the day for the victims, their families, and those treating them.

The Dean, the Very Revd Gary Hall, said, "All of us at Washington National Cathedral heard the news of this morning's shootings at the Washington Navy Yard with a mixture of shock and sadness. We mourn for those who have died, and we continue to grieve the persistence of gun violence in our nation."

The US Senate adjourned for the day in response to the shootings.

The Roman Catholic Archbishop for the Military Services, the Most Revd Timothy Broglio, said that the US had to "restore the notion of respect for life". He said that he had frequently visited the Navy Yard.

"Somehow we must restore the notion of respect for life into the fabric of the nation," he said. "When the uniqueness of the human person created in the image and likeness of God is universally recognised, the possibility of a mass shooting is more remote.

Saddleback pastor interviewed. The pastor of Saddleback Church, in California, the Revd Rick Warren, has spoken out after stepping out of the spotlight in response to his youngest son's suicide (News, 12 April).

In his first interview since his son's death, with Piers Morgan on CNN, Mr Warren said: "When I heard about those deaths, at the Navy Yard, the first thing I did was get down on my knees and pray for those families."

REUTERS

Witness: a demonstrator protests in Montreal against the Charter of Values proposed by the Quebec government. Published on Tuesday of last week, the charter would prohibit public employees from wearing "overt and conspicuous" religious symbols at work. The Bishop of Montreal, the Rt Revd Barry Clarke, argued that the charter could "foster prejudice and racism"

REUTERS

Crime scene: police stand guard at the Navy Yard on Tuesday

Swazi film depicts corruption

by Madeleine Davies

A NEW film about Swaziland, *The King and the People*, screened for the first time on Monday, provoked laughter in an audience that was well-versed in the corruption that is alleged to characterise life in the last remaining absolute monarchy in Africa.

The laughter reached its peak towards the end of the film, as the narrator summarised the extent of King Mswati III's powers: he appoints the Prime Minister, the cabinet, and judges; is head of the armed forces; and is "immune to the law".

The anger beneath the laughter became evident during the question-and-answer session that followed the screening, which was attended by many Swazis, including members of a pro-democracy group based in the UK, Swazi Vigil. They spoke of the lethargy of international organisations, and frustrated attempts to challenge the Foreign Office about the invitation to King Mswati to attend the Queen's Diamond Jubilee celebrations.

The film was shot undercover in Swaziland. It tells the story of the country through interviews with those fighting for a multi-party democracy. It contrasts the extravagance of the King, whose personal fortune is estimated at $200 million, with the destitution of the people.

Examples of his expenditure prompt comparisons to Marie Antoinette (in 2002, he spent $45 million on a private jet). In a country with the highest prevalence of HIV/AIDS in the world, the King violated his own law (a ban on sex with girls under 18) by taking a 17-year-old girl as his ninth wife.

The activists say that only mass mobilisation will bring change to the country. "Tradition is being used to manipulate the unsuspecting population," a leader of a teaching union warns.

Perhaps most powerful are the interviews with ordinary Swazis. One sugar-cane farmer describes how she brought up her grandchildren after her children were diagnosed with HIV/AIDS. "I want them to have a good life, and grow up well," she says.

On the day of the screening, Chatham House published a new report: *Swaziland: Southern Africa's Forgotten Crisis.* It highlights the world's lack of interest in a country with a "worrying" trajectory that the King and government ignore "at their peril".

Elections in Swaziland take place today. The Chatham House report suggests that the elections are likely to have little impact.

The King and the People was directed by Simon Bright of Zimmedia and will be shown at the Afrika Eye film festival in Bristol this year (www.afrikaeye.org.uk). Church groups can organise screenings through Action for South Africa (www.actsa.org).

"Immune to the law": King Mswati III

Anglican Communion gives thanks for Nigerian archbishop's release

By ACNS staff
Posted Sep 16, 2013

[Anglican Communion News Service] The Anglican Communion has given thanks to God for the safe release of the Church of Nigeria's second most senior cleric, Archbishop Ignatius Kattey.

Provincial Dean Kattey and his wife were kidnapped more than a week ago by armed men near their residence in the southern city of Port Harcourt. Mrs Kattey was later abandoned by the kidnappers. Kattey is the archbishop of Niger Delta Province and the bishop of Niger Delta North.

Statements of concern and prayers were issued around the Anglican Communion, not least from the Archbishop of Canterbury Justin Welby who has visited Nigeria many times.

According to police spokesperson Angela Agabe, Kattey was released by his captors at around 6.30 p.m. on Saturday, Sept. 14, behind a filling station at Eleme in Rivers State.

One news report stated that the Ven. Israel Omosioni, archdeacon of Eleme Archdeaconary, told Nigerian journalists that the archbishop was looking "hale and hearty" despite his ordeal.

Omosoni also revealed that his kidnappers had even given him N200 to to pay for his transport home.

From the moment the news broke on Saturday, members of the Anglican Communion expressed thanks and relief for the archbishop's safe return.

A statement on the archbishop of Canterbury's website said he "gave thanks" following the release of the Nigerian archbishop.

Bishop of Cameroon Dibo Elango wrote, "His Grace... is back home. We thank God Almighty. All Glory to the Lord, in the name of our Lord Jesus. Amen."

Suffragan Bishop of the Diocese in Europe, the Rt. Rev. David Hamid, said, "We give thanks for his freedom and return to his wife, family and church community."

Expression of thanks to God that the cleric had been returned safely also appeared on a range of social media sites from Anglicans and Episcopalians in countries including Canada, the U.S., England and across the African continent.

ACNS Anglican Communion
News Service

Home   Blogs   Africa   Asia   Americas   Europe & Middle East   Oceania   Other News   Actualités   Not

Home > Other News

Abp of Canterbury 'moved to tears' by visit of Abp Kattey

Posted on: October 4, 2013 4:06 PM

Photo Credit: Lambeth Palace

Related Categories: Abp Welby, Africa, Nigeria

From Lambeth Palace

The Archbishop of Canterbury has said that he was 'moved to tears' to welcome recently-released Nigerian archbishop Ignatius Kattey and his wife, Mrs Beatrice Kattey, to Lambeth Palace yesterday.

The Most Revd Ignatius Kattey, who is Dean and Archbishop of the Niger Delta Province, and Mrs Kattey were kidnapped on 6 September near their residence in the southern city of Port Harcourt. Mrs Kattey was released a few hours later, but Archbishop Kattey was held for more than a week.

Lambeth Palace staff lined the main staircase to applaud Archbishop and Mrs Kattey when they visited yesterday morning. They were accompanied their daughter, Josephine; Archdeacon John Chukwuemeka Adubasim, from the Diocese of Niger Delta North, who is on a study visit to the Diocese of Guildford; and Canon Ben Enwuchola, Chaplain to the Nigerian Congregation in London. They had tea with Archbishop Justin and then joined Lambeth Palace staff for Eucharist in the chapel, followed by lunch.

Speaking after the visit, Archbishop Justin said: "I was moved to tears to be able to welcome Archbishop Kattey and Mrs Kattey to Lambeth Palace after their ordeal, and to share Communion with us and all the staff. We rejoice at the love and grace of God which has renewed them in their freedom."

Archbishop Kattey said yesterday that he had come to Lambeth Palace to thank Archbishop Justin for calling on the church to pray for his release, and to express his thanks to those in the Church of England and the Anglican Communion for their prayers. "They prove that God answers prayers," he said.

Share   Tweet   Email

Archive   Search

152

Food goal is within reach, declares UN

by Madeleine Davies

A "FINAL PUSH" could enable the international community to meet the first Millennium Development Goal (MDG) — to halve, between 1990 and 2015, the proportion of people who suffer from hunger — a new report suggests.

The State of Food Insecurity in the World, published every year by the UN's Food and Agricultural Organisation (FAO), reports that about one in eight people in the world were estimated to be suffering from chronic hunger in 2011-13, a 17-per-cent reduction since 1990-92.

The authors write: "If the average annual decline of the past 21 years continues to 2015, the prevalence of undernourishment will reach a level close to the target. Meeting it would require considerable and immediate additional efforts."

The report notes that progress has not been universal. "Significant" progress has been achieved in East-ern and South Eastern Asia and Latin America, but one quarter of people in Sub-Saharan Africa are undernourished (down from 32.7 per cent in 1990). Last week, the government of Malawi and the UN launched a relief operation to help nearly 1.5 million in need of food aid in the country. Prolonged dry spells and decreased production have led to maize prices that are double those of last year.

Reasons for regional variation, say the authors, are food price inflation, political instability, lack of natural resources, economic growth, and public policy. Economic growth is not reaching its potential in rural Africa, it warns, because of "woe-fully inadequate infrastructure".

The authors highlight the importance of smallholder farmers, suggesting that targeting them can achieve hunger reduction "even where poverty is widespread". This has been demonstrated in Nicaragua, one of six countries studied in detail in the report.

Smallholders have been badly affected by sudden climate change, they warn, which "may play an even more prominent role in the coming decades". The volatility of food prices also makes these farmers "risk-averse, [it] lowers their propensity to adopt and invest in new technologies and ultimately results in lower overall production."

Globalisation is discussed. Remittances sent by migrants to their home countries now account for three times the amount of official development assistance, and has had "significant impacts on poverty and food security", the authors write.

The report suggests that the MDG target to halve the proportion of people living in extreme poverty was reached in 2008, and that the goal to halve the proportion without sustainable access to safe drinking water and basic sanitation was reached in 2010.

UN warns on Mali Three out of four households in Mali do not have enough to eat and are "heavily dependent on food assistance", the UN has warned. Last Friday, the World Food Programme announced that it was expanding its operation in the country, to reach more than 680,000 people in a country still recovering from civil conflict.

Targeting hunger: grain from the World Food Programme is distributed in Pibor, South Sudan, in July

Rich nations renege on debts

by Paul Wilkinson

SEVERAL developing countries are failing to meet international development goals, after rich nations reneged on pledges to deal with their debts, says a report published this week. Also, the debts of a number of EC states are increasing poverty at an alarming rate.

The study, *Life and Debt: Global studies of debt and resistance*, from the Jubilee Debt Campaign, examined nine countries: Egypt, El Salvador, Greece, Jamaica, Latvia, Pakistan, the Philippines, Portugal, and Tunisia.

It found that Jamaica spent 33 per cent of its revenue on foreign-debt repayments. The economy has not grown since 1990, and the number of women dying in childbirth has almost doubled in the past 20 years.

The debt crisis in Latvia, caused by the levels of borrowing taken out by its banks, forced more than 200,000 people to emigrate — the equivalent of six million people leaving the UK. Extreme poverty affects 31 per cent of the population.

Greece, which is now four years into a regime of austerity imposed by the IMF and the EU, spends 29 per cent of its revenue on foreign-debt repayments. Its economy has shrunk by 25 per cent.

Pakistan is spending 20 per cent of government revenue on debt payments. It is unlikely to meet many of the Millennium Development Goals (MDGs) set in 2000, in which rich nations committed themselves to resolving the debt problems of developing countries.

Tim Jones, a policy officer for the Jubilee Debt Campaign, said: "People in Jamaica, El Salvador, and Pakistan have suffered for over 30 years from debt resulting from reckless lending. IMF-imposed austerity has failed to reduce these debts, whilst the same imposed policies are now increasing poverty dramatically in Europe. Such unjust debts should be cancelled, as leaders committed to do at the mill.

A report calling for co-operation between lead developed and their development launched last.

Among its report sold munity show and quality attention to the implementation of duty and quota-free treatment for LDCs' exports.

At the same UN session, the EU and the UN's Food and Agriculture Organisation announced £50 million worth of agricultural projects, which should affect MDGs on hunger for two million people in Burkina Faso, Burundi, the Gambia, Haiti, Madagascar, and Mozambique.

Christian Aid praises progress

CHRISTIAN AID has welcomed a series of breakthroughs in discussions last week at the UN on what should replace the Millennium Development Goals (MDGs) in 2016, writes Paul Wilkinson.

The charity's Senior Adviser on Poverty and Inequality, Helen Dennis, warned, however, that there were still challenges ahead. She said last week: "The major breakthroughs include the recognition that all countries, including rich ones, should have to work towards the new goals, and that they should be only one set of goals covering both poverty and environmental protection.

"Also very welcome is the acceptance that, whilst all countries are responsible for protecting the environment, rich, high-consuming ones must do more. . .

"We will have to keep fighting for goals that drive the kind of structural transformation we want to see. The new goals could affect billions of people's lives, including those living in poverty in the UK; so getting them right could not be more important."

In a session of the UN General Assembly, however, several African ministers said that, while progress had been made, most were unlikely to achieve their MDGs by 2015.

The Congolese Minister of Foreign Affairs and La Francophonie, Basile Ikouébe, said that his country had made significant progress in education, and maternal and child health, but had delays in job-creation and the fight against poverty.

The President of Tanzania, Jakaya Mrisho Kikwete, claimed successes in universal primary education, reducing the prevalence of HIV/AIDS, and improving access to water and sanitation.

The President of Gambia, Yahya Jammeh, said that his country was on track to achieve its target for education. He surprised the assembly, however, when, in listing the three biggest threats to human existence, he included homosexuality, "which, though very evil, anti-human as well as anti-Allah, is being promoted as a human right by some powers".

Applause for Kattey

THE Archbishop of Canterbury has welcomed the Archbishop of Niger Delta Province in Nigeria, the Most Revd Ignatius Kattey, and his wife to Lambeth Palace, writes Madeleine Davies.

Archbishop Kattey was freed on last month (News, 20 September), more than a week after he was kidnapped by armed men, near his home in Port Harcourt. Archbishop Welby had published a prayer for his safe return just a day before his release was announced. Mrs Kattey was seized at the same time as her husband, but released hours later.

On their arrival last Friday, members of staff applauded them. Archbishop Kattey said that his release "proved that God answers prayers".

153

1

RESPECT FOR SECURITY AGENCIES

One day, during my kidnap, my kidnappers had wanted me to talk to my wife, Beatrice. But each time, my son, Dr Kattey Kattey, answered the call. That was my wife's phone number. That was very unusual. I accused them: 'You have killed my wife.' I felt that my wife may have died from trauma from all the events. She was no longer answering the calls. 'You see now, you have killed my wife.' I felt that Dr Kattey didn't want to tell me the sad story of my wife's death. Confidently, my kidnappers replied, 'Nothing happened to your wife. Your wife is well.' I again thought she might have been admitted into the hospital, but even at that, she should have been able to let me hear her voice.

After my release, my wife and Dr Kattey told me that both the Department of State Security Services and the police insinuated that my kidnappers had an insider collaborating with them. Let me make this point clear to anyone who cares to hear: the police, the Department of State Security (DSS), the armed forces, and in fact, all security agencies are well-trained and efficient. No one should ever joke with them or take them for granted. They can see you and size you up and, in most cases, will tell you your intentions. *If*, and I repeat, *if* they want to work and unravel mysteries that are humanly possible, they will do it. For example, if a policeman is missing—let's assume he is killed in the dark, in the dead of the night, in the remotest village and carried to another village and buried in a forest where no one except the killer has been before—police intelligence, the DSS, or the armed forces intelligence will locate the spot. Not only will they locate the spot, but they will make arrest(s) even if only one person carried out this monstrous act. That is, if they want to work. They are very efficient, and they are trained to do this type of work. But if in the church or mosque or in the open marketplace someone is killed, if they do not want to uncover the culprits, for years they will not, especially if people of importance or the government is behind the killing. They can have their hands tied.

As I said earlier, my wife and Dr Kattey said the security agencies told them that an insider was involved in my kidnap. They were right. It was an insider who was relaying to my kidnappers all that was happening at home. The kidnappers were aware of some persons who visited my residence. The insider was communicating with the kidnappers. After my release, based on the report of the security agencies, my wife summoned all our home staff: the security personnel at the gate, the domestic staff, the yardman, the drivers, and our personal staff. 'Daddy is an old man. The police and the DSS said an insider is involved in this kidnap. We treat all of you like our children. We don't treat you like workers. You eat what we eat, and we have never denied any of you food. When you have financial problems, we help you out. What on earth could make any one of you arrange or conspire to kidnap Daddy? You made an old man like this sleep in the bush for nine days.' One by one, every one of them denied it. 'Mummy, I don't know anything about this kidnap.' But one of the staff overdid the denial. He said, 'Mummy, I don't know anything about it. If I know anything about

Daddy's kidnap, let me not reach the age of forty. Let me die, and my wife and children should suffer.' I was present, along with all our domestic staff. Beatrice, during her speech, had said, 'Do you think the person who did this will reach the age of Daddy?'

This staff member was kneeling, with his two hands up, and swearing! He was the closest staff who was literally in contact with me every day. Wherever we went, he was with us over 90 per cent of the time. He was hard-working and most trusted. He had been in our service for about eighteen years. We financed his marriage. He had gained more from us than any other staff and was the most long-serving staff with us.

About a year later, this staff member just collapsed on duty. He was rushed to the hospital by his colleagues. He was pronounced dead. My wife and I were both worried and embarrassed. We immediately contacted Dr Atosemi Wokoma, one of the Diocese of Niger Delta North medical advisers, to help me arrange for an autopsy. We wanted to be sure of what transpired that caused this unexpected death. It was then that I learned that before an autopsy can take place, a member of the family of the deceased must consent to it. Unfortunately, his older brothers refused the autopsy, to our surprise. I tried to convince them that an autopsy would help the family. If there was any family disease, it would be revealed, and the family would be able to know how to tackle it. But all my explanations fell on deaf ears. They went back to their village. They suspected foul play. After a few days, they returned to us. In a meeting in my office, one of them, their spokesman, said, 'We have come to apologise on behalf of our brother and son who worked with you and is no more. There were many things he did not do right when he worked with you. We are sorry.' I then asked them, 'May we know what he did not do right?' They were silent. That question remains unanswered. The grapevine had it that, suspecting foul play, they had gone to consult a witch doctor to ascertain the cause of the death of their brother and son. They were told that his death was a repercussion of what he did to his master.

Let us go spiritual and mysterious now. You are free not to believe this. This dead worker has appeared to more than six persons in dreams, asking them to come and beg us to forgive him for the evil he did to us. King Solomon, the preacher, said this:

> Do not devise evil against your neighbor, for he dwells by you for safety sake; Do not strive with a man without cause, if he has done you no harm. (Proverb 3:29–30)

> Whoever rewards evil for good, evil will not depart from his house. (Proverbs 17:13)

David, the man after God's heart, had prayed thus.

> Do not keep silent, O God of my praise,

> For the mouth of the wicked and the mouth of the deceitful Have opened against me. They have spoken against me with a lying tongue.

> They have surrounded me with words of hatred. And fought against me without a cause.

> In return for my love, they are my accusers, But I give myself to prayer.

> They have rewarded me evil for good, And hatred for my love.

> Set a wicked man over him And let an accuser stand at his right hand

When he is judged, let him be found guilty, And let his prayer become sin.

Let his days be few, And let another take his office

Let his children be fatherless. And his wife a widow.

Let his children continually be vagabonds and beg. Let them seek their bread also from desolate places

Let the creditor seize all that he has, And let strangers plunder his labor

Let there be none to extend mercy to him, nor let there be any to favor his fatherless children.

Let his posterity b cut off, And in the generation following let their name be blotted out. (Psalm 109:1–13)

Lesson: We must be very careful not to do evil to those who have done us good. God will not take it kindly.

LEAVE THE COUNTRY

After my release, Hon. Magnus Abbey (now senator) paid us a visit. He immediately joined other well-meaning people in urging us to leave the country for some time, offering to pay for all flight expenses, first class, with any airline and to any country of our choice. Sir Abusemi Ngei, his aide, was sent to make all necessary arrangements for our travel.

It was during this journey that my wife, Beatrice; my daughter, Josephine (now Josephine Nwagbo); the Venerable John Adubasim, whom we sent on a study visit to the Diocese of Guilford; and the then Nigerian chaplain to the United Kingdom, Rev. Canon Ben

Enwuchola, paid a courtesy call to the Archbishop of Canterbury, His Grace, Most Rev. Justin Welby, the head of the Anglican Church worldwide. The reason for this visit was the principal role he played during the period of my kidnap. When he was told that my daughter, Josephine, was studying in Oxford, he sent a delegation led by Bishop Christopher Hills, the then Bishop of the Diocese of Guilford, to condole with her. He was also in contact with UK authorities on how to ensure I was released unhurt. We were well-received; the Lambeth Palace staff lined up the stairs to welcome us (visit YouTube for details). This was very humbling, and we sincerely thank the Archbishop and the palace staff for that honour. The Holy Eucharist and a sumptuous lunch were organised for us. The Archbishop also issued a prayer alert to the churches in the UK for our release. His special prayer for us is contained in the *Church Times* newspaper.

EPILOGUE

2

I FORGIVE YOU

One day, a lawyer walked into my office. He introduced himself as Ibikiri Otorubio, Esq., director of public prosecution, Rivers State Ministry of Justice.

He said he was handling my kidnap case. That was about five years after I was kidnapped. That was surprising to me because it was a matter that I had almost forgotten.

He wanted me in the court to testify in the matter. I felt there was no need to pursue that case again. However, many people, including my chancellor, Sir Barrister Emeka Ichoku, advised me to go to court. Never in my life had I been to court as a plaintiff, accused, or witness.

This was the document he gave to me:

CHARGE NO: PHC/ ---------/2015

THE STATE

VS.

1. CHIBUEZE NWAOGBA
2. ONYEDIKACHI EMMANUEL OKORO
3. PHILIP CHIKODIRI OGBUEWU

INFORMATION

AT THE SESSION HOLDEN AT PORT HARCOURT, on the ------- day of - --------- 2015, the Honourable Court is informed by the Honourable Attorney-General of Rivers State on behalf of the State that CHIBUEZE NWAOGBA, ONYEDIKACHI EMMANUEL OKORO and PHILIP CHIKODIRI OGBUEWU are charged with the following Offences:

STATEMENT OF OFFENCE – COUNT 1

CONSPIRACY TO COMMIT FELONY TO WIT, KIDNAPPING, Contrary to Section 516A (a) of the Criminal Code, Cap. 37, Vol. 2, Laws of the Rivers State of Nigeria, 1999.

PARTICULARS OF OFFENCE

CHIBUEZE NWAOGBA, ONYEDIKACHI EMMANUEL OKORO, PHILIP CHIKODIRI OGBUEWU with others at large on or about the 6th day of September, 2013 at Aleto Bridge, Eleme within the Port Harcourt Judicial Division did conspired and kidnapped the Most Reverend Ignatius C.O. Kattey, Archbishop of Niger Delta North Diocese and Dean of Anglican Communion.

STATEMENT OF OFFENCE – COUNT 2

CONSPIRACY TO COMMIT FELONY TO WIT, KIDNAPPING, Contrary to Section 516A (a) of the Criminal Code, Cap. 37, Vol. 2, Laws of the Rivers State of Nigeria, 1999.

PARTICULARS OF OFFENCE

CHIBUEZE NWAOGBA,ONYEDIKACHI EMMANUEL OKORO, PHILIP CHIKODIRI OGBUEWU with others at large on or about the 6th day of September, 2013 at Aleto Bridge, Eleme within the Port Harcourt Judicial Division did conspired and kidnapped one Mrs. Beatrice G. Kattey.

STATEMENT OF OFFENCE – COUNT 3

KIDNAPPING, Contrary to Section 1 (2) (b) of the Rivers State kidnap (Prohibition) Law No. 3 of 2009.

PARTICULARS OF OFFENCE

CHIBUEZE NWAOGBA,ONYEDIKACHI EMMANUEL OKORO, PHILIP CHIKODIRI OGBUEWU with others at large on or about the 6th day of September, 2013 at Aleto Bridge, Eleme within the Port Harcourt Judicial Division did kidnapped the Most Reverend Ignatius C.O. Kattey, Archbishop of Niger Delta North Diocese and Dean of Anglican Communion and unlawfully imprisoned him and thereafter demanded for ransom and was paid the sum of Ten Million Naira (N10,000,000.00) as ransom before his released.

STATEMENT OF OFFENCE – COUNT 4

KIDNAPPING, Contrary to Section 1 (2) (b) of the Rivers State kidnap (Prohibition) Law No. 3 of 2009.

PARTICULARS OF OFFENCE

CHIBUEZE NWAOGBA,ONYEDIKACHI EMMANUEL OKORO, PHILIP CHIKODIRI OGBUEWU with others at large on or about the 6th day of September, 2013 at Aleto Bridge, Eleme within the Port Harcourt Judicial Division did kidnap kidnapped one Mrs. Beatrice G. Kattey without her consent and unlawfully imprisoned her.

STATEMENT OF OFFENCE – COUNT 5

KIDNAPPING, Contrary to Section 1 (2) (b) of the Rivers State kidnap (Prohibition) Law No. 3 of 2009.

PARTICULARS OF OFFENCE

CHIBUEZE NWAOGBA,ONYEDIKACHI EMMANUEL OKORO, PHILIP CHIKODIRI OGBUEWU with others at large on or about the 13th day of February, 2013 at Aleto Bridge, Eleme within the Port Harcourt Judicial Division did kidnapped one Ukel Jerome Agba, and unlawfully imprisoned him and thereafter demanded for ransom and was paid the sum of Two Million Naira (N2,000,000.00) as ransom before his release.

STATEMENT OF OFFENCE – COUNT 6

KIDNAPPING, Contrary to Section 1 (2) (b) of the Rivers State kidnap (Prohibition) Law No. 3 of 2009.

PARTICULARS OF OFFENCE -

CHIBUEZE NWAOGBA,ONYEDIKACHI EMMANUEL OKORO, PHILIP CHIKODIRI OGBUEWU with others at large on or about the 15th day of February, 2013 at Pipeline, Aleto Eleme within the Port Harcourt Judicial Division did kidnapped one Mrs. Ann Agba and unlawfully imprisoned her and demanded for ransom and was paid the sum of Three Million Naira (N3,000,000.00) a ransom before her released.

STATEMENT OF OFFENCE – COUNT 7

CONSPIRACY TO COMMIT FELONY TO WIT, KIDNAPPING, Contrary to Section 516A (a) of the Criminal Code, Cap. 37, Vol. 2, Laws of the Rivers State of Nigeria, 1999.

PARTICULARS OF OFFENCE

CHIBUEZE NWAOGBA,ONYEDIKACHI EMMANUEL OKORO, PHILIP CHIKODIRI OGBUEWU with others at large on or about the 13th day of February, 2013 at Pipeline, Aleto Eleme within the Port Harcourt Judicial Division did conspired and kidnapped one Chidiebere Nwawuba.

STATEMENT OF OFFENCE – COUNT 8

KIDNAPPING, Contrary to Section 1 (2) (b) of the Rivers State kidnap (Prohibition) Law No. 3 of 2009.

PARTICULARS OF OFFENCE -

CHIBUEZE NWAOGBA,ONYEDIKACHI EMMANUEL OKORO, PHILIP CHIKODIRI OGBUEWU with others at large on or about the 15th day of February, 2013 at Pipeline, Aleto Eleme within the Port Harcourt Judicial Division did kidnapped one Chidiebere Nwawuba and unlawfully imprisoned him and demanded for ransom and was paid the sum of Two Million Naira (N2,000,000,00) a ransom before his released.

STATEMENT OF OFFENCE – COUNT 9

CONSPIRACY TO COMMIT FELONY TO WIT, KIDNAPPING, Contrary to Section 516A (a) of the Criminal Code, Cap. 37, Vol. 2, Laws of the Rivers State of Nigeria, 1999.

PARTICULARS OF OFFENCE

CHIBUEZE NWAOGBA,ONYEDIKACHI EMMANUEL OKORO, PHILIP CHIKODIRI OGBUEWU with others at large on or about the 12th day of December, 2012 at Ebubu, Eleme within the Port Harcourt Judicial Division did conspired and kidnapped one Doctor Lasisi Adebukola.

STATEMENT OF OFFENCE – COUNT 10

KIDNAPPING, Contrary to Section 1 (2) (b) of the Rivers State kidnap (Prohibition) Law No. 3 of 2009.

PARTICULARS OF OFFENCE

CHIBUEZE NWAOGBA,ONYEDIKACHI EMMANUEL OKORO, PHILIP CHIKODIRI OGBUEWU with others at large on or about the 12th day of December, 2012 at Ebubu, Eleme within the Port Harcourt Judicial Division did kidnapped one Doctor Lasisi Adebukola and unlawfully imprisoned him and demanded for ransom and was paid the sum of One Million Naira (N1,000,000.00) as ransom before his release.

STATEMENT OF OFFENCE – COUNT 11

CONSPIRACY TO COMMIT FELONY TO WIT, KIDNAPPING, Contrary to Section 516A (a) of the Criminal Code, Cap. 37, Vol. 2, Laws of the Rivers State of Nigeria, 1999.

4

PARTICULARS OF OFFENCE

CHIBUEZE NWAOGBA,ONYEDIKACHI EMMANUEL OKORO, PHILIP CHIKODIRI OGBUEWU with others at large on or about the 2nd day of May, 2012 at Sand Field Road, Aleto, Eleme within the Port Harcourt Judicial Division did conspired and kidnapped one Doctor Chidozie Fedelis Ezem.

STATEMENT OF OFFENCE – COUNT 12

KIDNAPPING, Contrary to Section 1 (2) (a) of the Rivers State kidnap (Prohibition) Law No. 3 of 2009.

PARTICULARS OF OFFENCE

CHIBUEZE NWAOGBA,ONYEDIKACHI EMMANUEL OKORO, PHILIP CHIKODIRI OGBUEWU with others at large on or about the 2nd day of May, 2013 at Sand Field Road, Eleme within the Port Harcourt Judicial Division did kidnapped one Doctor Chidozie Fidelis Ezem and unlawfully imprisoned him and demanded for ransom and was paid the sum of One Million, Three Hundred Naira (N1,300,000.00) as ransom before his release.

STATEMENT OF OFFENCE – COUNT 13

ATTEMPT TO KIDNAP, Contrary to Section 2 of the Rivers State kidnap (Prohibition) Law No. 3 of 2009.

PARTICULARS OF OFFENCE

CHIBUEZE NWAOGBA,ONYEDIKACHI EMMANUEL OKORO, PHILIP CHIKODIRI OGBUEWU with others at large on or about the 25th day of August, 2013 Opposite Winners Chapel Church, Elelenwo within the Port Harcourt Judicial Division attempted to kidnap one Honourable Fred Mbombo Igwe.

STATEMENT OF OFFENCE – COUNT 14

CONSPIRACY TO COMMIT FELONY TO WIT, KIDNAPPING Contrary to Section 516A (a) of the Criminal Code, Cap. 37, Vol. 2, Laws of the Rivers State of Nigeria, 1999.

PARTICULARS OF OFFENCE

CHIBUEZE NWAOGBA,ONYEDIKACHI EMMANUEL OKORO, PHILIP CHIKODIRI OGBUEWU with others at large on or about the 17th day of May, 2013 near

5

Eleme Forest within the Port Harcourt Judicial Division did conspired and kidnapped one Engr. Bernard Azubuike Ezem.

STATEMENT OF OFFENCE – COUNT 15

KIDNAPPING: Contrary to Section 1 (2) (b) of the Rivers State kidnap (Prohibition) Law No. 3 of 2009.

PARTICULARS OF OFFENCE

CHIBUEZE NWAOGBA, ONYEDIKACHI EMMANUEL OKORO, PHILIP CHIKODIRI OGBUEWU with others at large on or about the 7th day of May, 2013 near Eleme Forest within the Port Harcourt Judicial Division did kidnapped one Engr. Bernard Azubuike Ezem and unlawfully imprisoned him and demanded for ransom and was paid the sum of Eight Hundred Thousand Naira (N800,000.00) as ransom before his release.

STATEMENT OF OFFENCE – COUNT 16

CONSPIRACY TO COMMIT FELONY TO WIT, KIDNAPPING: Contrary to Section 516A (a) of the Criminal Code, Cap. 37, Vol. 2, Laws of the Rivers State of Nigeria, 1999.

PARTICULARS OF OFFENCE

CHIBUEZE NWAOGBA, ONYEDIKACHI EMMANUEL OKORO, PHILIP CHIKODIRI OGBUEWU with others at large on or about the 31st day of May, 2013 at Aleto Bridge by Petro-Chemical, Eleme within the Port Harcourt Judicial Division did conspired and kidnapped one Iheakanwah Felix Arinze.

STATEMENT OF OFFENCE – COUNT 17

KIDNAPPING, Contrary to Section 1 (2) (a) of the Rivers State kidnap (Prohibition) Laws No. 3 of 2009.

PARTICULARS OF OFFENCE

CHIBUEZE NWAOGBA, ONYEDIKACHI EMMANUEL OKORO, PHILIP CHIKODIRI OGBUEWU with others at large on or about the 31st day of May, 2013 at Aleto Bridge by Petro-Chemical, Eleme within the Port Harcourt Judicial Division did kidnapped one Iheakanwah Felix Arinze and unlawfully imprisoned him and demanded for ransom and was paid the sum of One

6

Million, Eight Hundred Thousand Naira (N800,000.00) as ransom before his released.

STATEMENT OF OFFENCE – COUNT 18

ARMED ROBBERY, Contrary to Section 1 (2) (a) and (b) of the Robbery and Firearms (Special Provisions) Act, Cap. RII, Laws of the Federation of Nigeria, 2010.

PARTICULARS OF OFFENCE

CHIBUEZE NWAOGBA, ONYEDIKACHI EMMANUEL OKORO, PHILIP CHIKODIRI OGBUEWU with others at large on or about the 31st day of May, 2013 at Aleto Bridge by Petro-Chemical, Eleme within the Port Harcourt Judicial Division did robbed one Iheakanwah Felix Arinze of the sum of Two Hundred and Fifty Thousand Naira (N250,000.00) one Samsung Galaxy Sim handset, Three (3) bottles of perfumes, one Samsung Galaxy Note 101 handset, one HP Laptop and Three (3) pairs of shoes.

STATEMENT OF OFFENCE – COUNT 19

ARMED ROBBERY, Contrary to Section 1 (2) (a) and (b) of the Robbery and Firearms (Special Provisions) Act, Cap. RII, Laws of the Federation of Nigeria, 2010.

PARTICULARS OF OFFENCE

CHIBUEZE NWAOGBA, ONYEDIKACHI EMMANUEL OKORO, PHILIP CHIKODIRI OGBUEWU with others at large on or about the 2nd day of May, 2013 at Sand Field Road, Aleto Bridge by Petro-Chemical, Eleme within the Port Harcourt Judicial Division did robbed one Doctor Fidelis Chidozie Ezem of his Toyota Camry Car.

I.OTORUBIO, ESQ.,
Director of Public Prosecutions,
For: Honourable Attorney-General,
Rivers State.

7

168

IN THE HIGH COURT OF RIVERS STATE OF NIGERIA
IN THE PORT HARCOURT JUDICIAL DIVISION
HOLDEN AT PORT HARCOURT

CHARGE NO: PHC/ ---------/2015

THE STATE

VS.

1. CHIBUEZE NWAOGBA
2. ONYEDIKACHI EMMANUEL OKORO
3. PHILIP CHIKODIRI OGBUEWU

LIST OF PROSECUTION WITNESSES

1. MOST. REV. IGNATIUS C.O. KATTEY
2. MRS. BEATRICE G. KATTEY
3. DR. LASISI ADEBUKOLA
4. IHEAKANWAH FELIX AZINZE
5. HONOURABLE FRED MBOMBO IGWE
6. DR. FIDELIS CHIGOZIE EZEM
7. CHIDIEBERE NWAWUBA
8. UKEL JEROME AGBA
9. HUMPHREY OHIKHUARE
10. REUBEN UZOMA
11. DESMOND ADAMU
12. FRIDAY EZEGBUNA

INFORMATION

DATED THIS --------2ND-------- DAY OF ---OCT.--- 2015

FILED THIS ---------------------------- DAY OF ---------------- 2015.

I.OTORUBIO, ESQ.,
Director of Public Prosecutions,
For: Honourable Attorney-General,
Rivers State.

THE JUDICIARY
HIGH COURT REGISTRY
PORT HARCOURT
CASH OFFICE
Date 2/10/2015

8

169

PROOF OF EVIDENCE

STATEMENT OF WITNESSES

1. **MOST. REV. IGNATIUS C.O. KATTEY**

My name is Ignatius Kattey on Friday 6th September, 2013 I was travelling with my wife to Port Harcourt from Eleme at about 10-11pm.

We were confronted by a group three young men. They pull out my driver from the vehicle and one of them took the driver's seat, another sat by me and the other sat in front at the right side of the driver. We were driven into the bush for about two kilometers our bags were searched and all the money was to removed or taken from us. Then we were taken to the bush, perhaps a transit camp. I pleaded with them to released my wife, which they obliged.

From then on till Saturday 14th September, 2013 when I was released, I was sleeping in the bush under rain and sunshine. Sometimes, two or three persons were on guard but on the whole, they were not less than six persons I preached to them sometime but I was not allowed to see their faces since I was always facing the bush and they were always behind me.

However, I told them I had forgiven them but advised them not to continue with this their business of kidnapping.

2. **MRS. BEATRICE G. KATTEY**

I am Mrs. Beatrice Kattey a native of Alode Eleme from Eleme Local Government Area. I am the wife of Most Rev. Ignatius C.O. Kattey, the Bishop of the Diocese of Niger Delta North, Archibishop of Niger Delta and the Dean of the Church of Nigeria Anglican Communion.

My husband and I were on our way ot Port Harcourt on the 6th of September 2013 when a gang of men stopped our car at gun point, dragged the driver down, entred the car collected the money and other valuable on us and dorve the car to the bush. On arrival to a point they ordered us out of car and walked us into the bush. After a long trek, I fell down at a point, could not walk strong again. They were saying they will shoot my leg if I don't walk fast. I managed to walk with the help of my husband who supported me. As we got to a point, we were asked to sit on the ground to have a little rest. It was at this point that my husband pleaded with them to allow me to go back. They accepted and showed me the direction to get out of the bush. I pleaded that they should give me my cell phone they then removed my sim card and put into one of their phones and gave me.

I walked alone in the bush and got out, after which the police the JTF, my family and church members met me and took me home. In the morning I was told that the police took the car to the Eleme Police Station, so in the Company of my family and others I went to the station, gave my report and collected the car and other property from the D.P.O.

3. **DR. LASISI ADEBUKOLA**
I Pastor Dr. Lasisis Adebukola of Dorkson Medical Clinics No. 215 Old Bori Road, Abbofia, Ebubu were and the seeing answer of Rhema Pentecostal Assembly International Ministry was returning home on Wednesday 12th of December, 2012 when suddenly a red mecedez Benz car 190 double crossed my car (Pilot Jeep) at came out with AK 47 Riffle I was ordered into my boot and taken to a thick forest after six days I was released after a ransom of 1 million naira was paid in the night at about 9pm.
After released one them who claimed to calling with phone No. 08098484172, 07060777164. I saw Chibueze Nwagwa, Philip Ogbue crossing who confessed they did the kidnapping with one Carpet and were begging for pardon.

4. **IHEAKANWAH FELIX AZINZEH**
My names are Iheakanwah Felix Anizeh. I am a native of Umuakah, Njaba Local Government Area, Imo State I live at the above stated address and I work with Zenith Bank Plc, at 126 Ikwerre Road, Port Harcourt, Rivers State. I am married with a daughter I was abducted by the Suspects on 31/05/2013 on my way from my former branch at Zenith Bank, Onne, I was driving on Aleto Bridge by Petrochemical when the Suspects opened fire at my car. In that context, I had to stop fear that they might kill me if I don't I was taken to a nearby bush at gun point and I was asked to describe the placed in the car were I kept monies. They took from my car, two hundred and fifty thousand naira,

10

Samsung Galaxy Sim, three (3) bottles of perfumes, Samsung Galaxy note 101 and three pair of shoes and a HP Laptop. After shooting and taking my belonging from the car. We trekked from about 8.30pm to about 2.30pm when one of them whom I perceived to be leader called another person to bring a car at a particular point. We drove for about 20 mins and trekked for another 30 mins to a thick forest. The next day being Saturday (01/06/13) they asked for my wife's and mother's number and called them to bring Ten Million Naira before I will be released. On Sunday (02/06/13) my wife dropped N300.000 for them (suspects) along Ogoni Road before leaving to collect the ransom, they told me they will also kidnap my wife (they insisted my wife should be the person to deliver the first ransom. I was pleading and crying for days until they accepted to accept One Million, five Hundred Thousand Naira only which they collected at Onne New Road on the Seventh day of my hostage (on a Thursday) my car which was left on the bridge (Aleto) was stolen and was recovered in Ndiolumber in Isialangwa, Abia State. They suspects in the custody Department of State Security have been identified by me and they have also confessed to kidnapping me and some others and collected ransoms.

5. HONOURABLE FRED MBOMBO IGWE
On the 25th day of August, 2013 I was home (Eleme) to visit some of my friends and Associates whose wives gave birth. They also named their children after me as our custom requires. After I furnished with them we branched the NNPC (EPCL) Life Camp where our friend of mine who to followed me on this trip lives. At about 8pm that evening we left him and headed for Port Harcourt via the Eleme/Elelenwo axis of the East/West Road. As we got to a yet another bad spot on the road, opposite the Winners Chapel Church, Elelenwo, two gun men emerged out of the darkens in front of a filing station and started shooting at the car, we were travelling with. In the ensuring confussion I was able to instruct my young friend, Mr. Paul Idedia who was driving me to speed off and never to stop. He continued to speed away from the attack and never stopped. After we passed the Railway Bridge, still at Elelenwo, I noticed that I was bleeding from the top of my head. Consequently, I directed my friend to a nearby hospital – Shawsand Medical Centre – around vicinity of Eleme Junction (Kilometer 14, Aba, Port Harcourt Express Way, Port Harcourt. I

11

was treated there and later discharged. The following day, 26.08/2013, I reported to the police at Elelenwo Road, Police Division within the Jurisdiction of the attack and the matter was later transferred at their own instance to SARS (Special Anti Robbery Squad) Rukpoku for further reaction,. The shooting left bullet holes on my said car, a toyota corolla with Reg. No. GCG11. The glass at the back was also completely shattered.

6. **DR. FIDELIS CHIGOZIE EZEM**
I am Dr. Ezem Fidelis Chidozie from Amawom Owerri Municipal Council, Imo State. A graduate of veterinary Medicine. Usman Danfodio University, Sokoto. I am a Private veterinary surgeon. The Director of Molars Veterinary Services Ltd, Woji, Port Harcourt.
On the 2nd of May, 2013 around 9.00pm, two gun men abducted me about 10 meres from the gate of my residential house at Sand field Road, Aleto Eleme with my black Toyota Camry 2003 Model, Engine No. 7253203, Chassis No. 4T1BE32K8ZU-097885. The armed bandits forced me into the boot of my car after taking some amount of money from me and drove to unknown area near a thick forest when they stopped the car, they opened the boot and ordered my into the forest with their AK 47 riffle. After walking for about 30 minutes into the forest, they ordered me to remove my shoes. I was blind folded with a fabric with legs and hand tied, I was layed on the floor. Meanwhile, my wife called me on my phone, they gang of about eight told her that they are kidnappers she should arrange for ten million naira ransom for my release. My younger brother Engr. Bernard Azuwuike Ezem came to Port Harcourt the following day being 3rd of May, 2013 to negotiate for my release. My wife sent about N500,000.00 to them on the 4th of May, 2013 at a designated area in Onne Eleme on the 7th of May, 2013 my younger brother sent the sum of Eight Hundred Thousand Naira (N800,000 to the kidnappers for my release after which he was abducted the kidnapers numbering about eight now released me after abducting my brother. They told me that I their main target, I should bring One Million Naira, (N1, 000,000.00) for them to released my younger brother. On the 10th of May, 2013 about 11.00pm I took about N800,000.00 ransom to them in an unfinished house in Onne for my brothers released. My brother was released about 3 hours after they collected the money from me.

12

My black Toyota Camry car has never been found, uptill now that am writing this report. One of the kidnapers called me with this number 07060777164, telling me to scratch a N25,000.00 recharge card for me so that he will show me the way about my Toyota Camry car. I actually sent the N25,000 MTN card for him. He described to me where I can located the car but the car was nowhere to be found.

7. **CHIDIEBERE NWAWUBA**
    I am a native of Umuankwa Emi Owerri North Local Government in Imo State, I am a driver I am attached with Mobil, I attend Progressive Primary School Umuanwaka Emii Owerri North. I attend Comprehensive Secondary School Alesa Eleme, I was adopted along side with my Oga Mr. U.J. Agba on our way back from the Church on 13/2/2013 ash Wednesday when the adopted us the. They also adopted my Oga's wife Mrs. Ann Agba when she came for the ransom, I and my oga Mr. Ukel Jerome Agba was relised.
    On the 31th/10/13 I, Chidiebere Nwawuda and my Oga Mr. Ukel Jerome Agba was invited to SSS Office when we were going road for paraded and identification I identified one of them by his hight and his voice, he was the one that ask us to go and get more money and I was made to know that his name is Chibueze Nwaogba by SSS.

8. **UKEL JEROME AGBA**
    I, Ukel Jerome Agba 53 of G113 Intels Aba Road Camp, Port Harcourt was kidnapped on 13 February 2013 at about 2000hrs at Pipeline, Aleto Eleme while returning from Ash Wednesday Mass in Company of Chidiebere Nwamba a driver with my company. We were initially robed and later bundled into my car and taken to a point where we were brought down and taken through the bush for about one and half hours until we got to a location close to some Indian bamboo and detained. Contact was made with my landlord who informed my company and report made to the police, my car was abandoned opposite Ecobank Eleme and recovered by my colleague the next day while going to work. I was released on 15th February, 2013 after a ransom of N2m was paid by my wife who brought the money was detained for another 3 nights until additional N3m was paid. She was

13

released on 18 Feb 2013. I made statements at Anti-Kidnap Unit of the Police at Moscow Road and was debriefed by Director DSS PH. I have not heard from the Security Agencies until today but during this time, several persons were also kidnapped by the same gang. I cannot recognize all the gang members except the marks man with AK 47 AND Mohammed, the one who guarded us. I presumed there are about 7 to 8 members of this gang and location is general area of AP Filling Station near Eleme Refinery Junction. The marksman is about 5" 4", dark, speaks Ibo of Emene dialect according to my driver who is Ibo I suspect he is a dismissed regiment from the military.

9.	HUMPHREY OHIKHUARE	⎫ Security Operatives with the
10.	REUBEN UZOMA	⎪ Department of State Security
11.	DESMOND ADAMU	⎬ Services (SSS) who investigated
12.	FRIDAY EZEGBUNA	⎭ this matter. To state their findings during the trial.

14

<u>STATEMENT OF ACCUSED PERSONS</u>

1. <u>CHIBUEZE NWAOGBA</u>
    I Chibueze Nwogba wish to make a statement. I want someone to
    write down what I will say. I have been told that I need not say
    anything unless I wish to do so and that whatever is ay may be given
    in evidence. I wish to state as follows that I am Chibueze Nwogba, a
    native of Amajim-Amuika in Izza South Local Government Area of
    Ebonyi State. I was born into the family of Mr. and Mrs. Nwogba Ugo I
    am twenty eight year and a Christian by religion. I have two children
    and married to Joy Chibueze. I attended Community Primary School
    Amajim Umuika, Ebonyi State in 1996 and dropped out in Primary Six
    (6) because of lack of Finance to further my education. I am a
    professional mechanic and work at refinery road, Eleme, Port Harcourt.
    I started kidnapping in 2012 and since then I have been involved in
    several kidnapping activities and petty armed robbery. I was
    introduced into kidnapping job by one Oke Nwaburu from Enugu State.
    I met him at a place in refinery road, Eleme, where we smoke Indian
    hemp. Before I went into fulltime kidnapping I used to join some boys
    to do breaking and entry at Akpajo area and Eleme. I had gone to
    prison in 2010 on Awaiting Trial over stealing and armed robbery and I
    spent one week in Port Harcourt prison. In my kidnapping gang, we
    are about seven with the following boys, Oke Mwanburu, Philip, an
    elderly man we call carpet a Fulani boy called Buhari, one Oyedikachi
    and face, I went with my gang members to kidnap one Fidelis Eze, a
    vertinary doctor who leaves at Eleme. It was Okey Nwanburu that
    brought the kidnap job of Fidelis Ezem Okey told us that he use to see
    the man with flashy cars and that when we kidnap him, he will be able
    to pay huge amount of money. I cannot remember the exact month
    we kidnapped the vertinary doctor but it was this year 2013 we went
    to his house at Eleme to kidnap him I was the one that drove the
    man's vehicle with which we kidnapped him. We collected one Million
    Five Hundred Thousand Naira of that kidnap. We took him to Eleme
    bush where we kept him until the ransom was payed. Another person
    we kidnapped at the Eleme Bridge was one Zenith Bank staff called
    Arinze. We kidnapped him when he was driving pass the road and took
    him into Eleme bush and he pay a ransom of One Million Five Hundred
    Thousand Naira which we collected at Onne in a jungle. We made an
    attempt to kidnap one Igwe Fred whom I latter was told is a
    Commissioner for Sports in Rivers State. The attempt to kidnap the
    Commissioner failed because when we flagged him down in his car to
    stop at the Eleme Bridge, he refused and sped off, when he refused to
    stop, Oke Nwaburu fired him but he still sped off. We did not do any
    kidnap job that day again because we were afraid that the man may

15

:   :

176

come back with police to that Eleme bridge to arrest us. Normally, when we kidnap any person, we instruct the old man, face Oyedikachi and Buhari to guard the victims. On the 6th of September 2013 I and members of my gang kidnapped one Bishop Ignatius C.O. Kattey at the Eleme Bridge when he was driving through we flagged him to stop and when he did, we kidnapped him and allowed his driver to go we then took him deep into the Eleme Bridge. It was later we heard he was an Archbishop. We actually kidnapped him with his wife but he pleaded with us to allow his wife to go and we allowed the wife to go on the ground that she was going to get us money. The man told us that he is a Bishop but we told him that we cannot let him go since we have kidnapped him already. It is Oke that normally do the negotiation for ransom and we collected Ten Million Naira ransom for the kidnap of the Archbishop. I collected three million as my share of the ransom that was paid. We gave Oyedikachi Five Hundred Thousand and Naira we gave Face One Million Naira but Philip collected Two Hundred and Fifty Thousand Naira from Face's share by force, Philip collected Two Million Seven Hundred Thousand Nara as his share, Oke collected Two Million, Seven Hundred Thousand Naira while we share the rest among other members of our gang.

We also kidnapped one Uke Jerome on 13th of February 2013 around 12midnight at the same Eleme Bridge. He was driving with one, young man when we came out from the bush and ask him to stop. He stop and we kidnapped him and the boy, that was driving him. We took him into the Eleme Forest and later paid the Sum of Five Million Naira which we shared among ourselves. It was his wife that brought the initial two Million naira which Oke collected but later released the man and his driver and held the man's wife back. We told the man to give us additional three million naira if he wants his wife to be release and he paid us the additional three million before we released the wife. I can also remember that we kidnapped a Yoruba pastor whom I don't know his name. we stopped his vehicle and discovered that he was with three other old men. He told us that he is a pastor and that he was coming from the hospital but Philip said he is not just a pastor but a rich doctor. He then allowed the three other old men to go and we carried the Yoruba man deep into the Eleme forest. He paid us the sum of Three Hundred Thousand Naira which was delivered by his wife but I later collected another three hundred thousand naira from her along the Eleme Express way. All the victims we kidnapped at the Eleme Alato Bridge, we do it at night to present us from being seen and then the road would have been lonely and its only few vehicles that will be driving pass. The red mecezed benz I bought with the money I made from mechanic work we used it to block doctor Lasisi

16

when we kidnapped him at Obubu in Eleme. I bought a Camry Toyota car for Nine Hundred Thousand Naira and Fifty Thousand naira (N950,000). The money I used I buying the Camry car was my own share of the ransom we collected from Pastor Ignatius Kattey. The car has registration number BWY 203 AR. Also, I bought a land at Umudino, Oyigbo West Oyigbo Local Government Area for the sum of One Million Five Hundred Thousand Naira (N1.5m) the money I used in buying the land was the ransom I got from both Jerome Agba and one Zenith bank worker Arinze Felix. I Chibueze Nwogba, I have read the above statement and I have been told that I can correct, alter or add anything I wish. This statement is true; I have made it of my own freewill.

2. **ONYEDIKACHI EMMANUEL OKORO**

I Onyedikachi Emmanuel Okoro wish to make a statement I want someone to write down what I say. I have been told that I need not say anything unless I wish to do so and whatever I say may be given in evidence. I am Onyedikachi Emmanuel Okoro, a native of Ihiteafor-Ukwu Community in Ezinihite Mbaise Local Government Area of Imo State. I am Twenty Six (26) years old and first son of Mr. Friday Okoro and Mrs. Ngozi Okoro I never attended any formal education but I learnt shoe making business from oga cos at Power line, Amama market Aba in1998 and I served him for one year. After serving oga cos I travelled back to the village before I relocated to Enugu to do wheel barrow pushing business for about one year. I also travelled to Abuja where I got, a job as a mechanic operator in a pure water factory while I was in Abuja around Kaduna road I met Ifesinachi also known as face and Chibueze Nwogba also known as Pastor Ifesinachi was automobile electrician while Pastor was a trailer mechanic. I came to Port Harcourt in 2005 and got a job at Izzi table water around oil mill, Aba Road as mechanic operator. I worked for one year at Izzi table water before I went to learn bore drilling business with Samson, a native of Benue State, I worked with Samson for two years before I left to stay on my won at No. 10 Emine Avenue Elelenwo. About two years ago, Ifesinachi called on phone and requested that I trace the way about of Chibueze Nwagbe at Eleme refinery and I went and saw him when I met Chibueze Nwogba at Refinery, he told me that he is into condensate fuel business and that he needed money to run the business, as a result of the discussion, I called Ifesinachi who was in Abuja and he brought thirty or forty thousand naira and we gave it to Chibueze. Chibueze Squandered the money and told us that the business failed. Sometime, last year I met Chibueze at Eleme Junction and explained to him that I need financial assistance he gave me one thousand (N1000) and promised to help me later, after sometime

17

come back with police to that Eleme bridge to arrest us. Normally when we kidnap any person, we instruct the old man, face Oyedikachi and Buhari to guard the victim. On the 6th of September, 2013 I and members of my gang kidnapped one Bishop Ignatius C.O. Kattey at the Eleme Bridge when he was driving through we flagged him to stop and when he did, we kidnapped him and allowed his driver to go we then took him deep into the Eleme bridge. It was later we heard he was an Archbishop. We actually kidnapped him with his wife but he pleaded with us to allow his wife to go and we allowed the wife to go on ground that she was going to get us money. The man told us that he is Bishop but we told him that we cannot let him go since we have kidnapped him already. It is Oke that normally do the negotiation for ransom and we collected Ten Million Naira ransom for the kidnap of the Archbishop. I collected Three Million as my share of the ransom that was paid. We gave Oyedikachi Five Hundred Thousand and Naira we gave Face One Million from Face's share by force, Philip collected Two Million Seven Hundred Thousand Naira as his share, Oke collected Two Million, Seven Hundred Thousand Naira while we share the rest among other members of our gang.

We also kidnapped one Uke Jerome on 13th of February, 2013 around 12 midnight at the same Eleme Bridge. He was driving with one young man when we came out from the bush and ask him to stop. He stop and we kidnapped him and the boy, that was driving him. We took him into the Eleme Forest and alter paid the Sum of Five Million Naira which we shared among ourselves. It was his wife that brought the initial Two Million Naira which Oke collected but later released the man and his driver and held the man's wife back. We told the man to give us additional Three Million Naira if he wants his wife to be released and he paid us the additional Three Million before we released the wife. I can also remember that we kidnapped a Yoruba pastor whom I don't know his name. We stopped his vehicle and discovered that he was with three other old men. He told us that he is a pastor and that he was coming from the hospital but Philip said he is not just a pastor but a rich doctor. He then allowed the three other old men to go and we carried the Yoruba man deep into the Eleme Forest. He paid us the sum of Three Hundred Thousand Naira which was delivered by his wife but I later collected another Three Hundred Thousand Naira form her along the Eleme Express Way. All the victims' we kidnapped at the Eleme Aleto Bridge, we do it at night to prevent us from being seen and then the road would have been lonely and its only few vehicles that will be driving pass. The red Mercedes Benz I bought with the money I made from mechanic work we used it to block doctor Lasisi some last year I called on phone and he asked me to come to a

18

mechanic workshop at Eleme junction and when I got there he showed me a bus and I requested to drive it for him in order to support myself, he doubted my abilities to drive and refused. Later one electrician took the bus to Akpajo and had some problems with the car, Chibueze was angry and decided to collect bus from the electrician and I assisted him in driving the bus to where it was repaired and the bus engine replaced with a new one. He now realized that I can drive but insisted that I should get a driver while I will serve as a conductor and I started the bus business from there. After two months, the bus developed another fault, he decided to collect the bus from us. When he collected the bus from me I begged him to introduced me into his business which he refused initially but after much pressure he opened up to me and said that if I am interested I should help him to look after kidnapped victims whenever he and his gang abduct them. I accepted because I was jobless. The first kidnap job I helped him to look after the kidnapped victim was that of Zenith Bank Staff, Arinze, earlier this and I and two other gang members namely Ifesinachi and the Fulani man whose real name I don't know held the victim hostage inside Eleme Forest for Five or Six days at the end of the operation, Chibueze gave me Fifty Thousand Naira as my share and did not tell me how much he collected as ransom. The second kidnap job we did together is the Archbishop Ignatius Kattey's kidnap. The member of our gang that kidnapped the Archbishop are Chibueze Nwogba, Okey, Philip, myself, Ifesinachi, the Fulani man and old Igbo man that I do not know his real name. Those that abducted the Archbishop on the road as Chibueze Nwogba, Okey and Philip and they have one riffle while me, Ifesinachi, the Fulani man and old Igbo man took care of the Bishop inside Eleme Forest. At the end of the Archbishop operation, Chibueze gave me Five Hundred Thousand Naira (N500,000.00) as my share. I used this money to reroof my mother's house in the village. The leader of the gang is Chibueze followed by Okey and Philip and they are the ones that negotiate and give order on the release of our kidnapped victims. Okey was responsible for the negotiation of the ransom payment of the Archbishop.

3. PHILIP CHIKODIRI OGBUEWU
I Ogbewu Philip Chikodiri wish to make a statement. I want someone to write down what I say. I have been told that I need not say anything unless I wish to do so and that whatever I say may be given in evidence. I am Ogbewu Philip Chikodirin a native of Ochukwuagbe in Ezza South Local Government Area of Ebonyi State. I am Thirty Five (35) years old and a mechanic by profession. I was born into the family of Mr. and Mrs. Ogbewu Nweke. I leave in Port Harcourt with my wife Blessing Philip whom I married in the year 2006. We leave at

19

Refinery Road by A.P. Filling Station, a road behind United Bank for African UBA. I am a Christian by religion and I attended Ndembie primary School in my village at Ochukwagba community. I stopped my education at Primary school level because of financial problems and the death of my father. I was introduced into kidnapping in 2012 by Chibueze Nwogba and one other man we normally call carpet. It was Charles I knew first before Chibueze. I used to know Carpet as Charles, it was later I know he was called Carpet. He introduced me to Chibueze I know carpet when I was selling fuel and diesel at refinery road. Carpet called me in 2012 and told me to join his gang so that I can get good money, it was then he introduced me to Chibueze and I was told that the business they are involved in is kidnapping that was how I started kidnapping with Charles and Chibueze when I went into kidnapping in2012, I knew some other people who are members of our gang. The people that joined us in the kidnapping business are Oke, Oyedikachi, one Hausa boy called Danfulaini and one other guy called face (Ifesinachi) the kidnap I did with these people was the kidnap of one Medical Doctor at Abubu whom we kidnapped immediately he left his clinic. We monitored him before we kidnapped him it was Carpet (Charles) that brought the job to kidnap the Doctor as he told us that the man was not just a pastor but a rich Doctor. It was Ifeanyi we instructed to monitor the Doctor, Lasisi Adekunle. I was the one that drove the vehicle with which we kidnapped the Doctor and we then took him to Eleme bush and kept him for six (6) days after, we called his people to bring money for us before we release him. He paid a ransom of One million Five Hundred Thousand Naira (N1.5m). I also was involved in the kidnap of one Zenith Bank Staff, Felix Arinze whom we also took to the bush and collected one million five hundred thousand naira. I was given the sum of one hundred and fifty thousand naira. It is Chibueze that is the leader of our gang followed by Oke and Carpet and them me. I used to sometime guard the victim of our kidnap in the bush with Onyedikcahi Danfulani, Face and Carpet. I have also joined my group in the kidnap of one man. I think he is a Calabar man, we kidnapped him with his driver and when his wife brought the ransom, we held the wife and released the man and his driver with the instruction to go and get more money before we would released his wife. We held the wife when he brought two million naira for the husband's release and after we released the man, he later brought three million naira for the release of his wife. The Calabar man called Jerome Agba pleaded with us that we should release his wife since he has paid us two million but Oke insisted that he must pay three million before his wife will be released to him. We also made all attempt to kidnap the Commissioner of Sports, Rivers State, Mr. Fred Mbombo Igwe but the attempt failed as the

20

commissioner refused to stop is vehicle when we stopped him. Oke later fired at him several shots when he observed that the man was not ready to stop after the incident it was later we knew he was a Commissioner for Sports. On 6th September 2013 at that Aleto Bridge in Eleme Road, we kidnapped one Ignatius C.O. Kattey and his wife and when the man pleaded with us to release his wife and go with him, we did. We released the wife and asked her to go and get money for the release of his wife. We kept him for nine days in the bush. When we kidnapped him we instructed Danfulani, Face, Oyedikachi and Carpet to watch over him but I sometime go to the bush to see my people and the Bishop. Before we released the Bishop, he paid us Ten Million Naira (N10m) as ransom. It was myself and Oke that went to collect the ransom at Trailer Park Road, along Onne when we collected the money, we shared it amongst ourselves Chibueze took three (3) million naira (N3m) Oke collected two million five hundred naira only (N2.5m) I called two million five hundred naira only (N2.5m) we gave Oyedikachi Five hundred thousand naira (N500,000) we also shared the money to other members of our gang including Carpet. I paid One Million Naira into my wife Blessing's account. The account number has the sum of five hundred thousand naira before I paid in the one million. The five hundred thousand naira in the account was the money I got from previous kidnap operation I did with my gang. Although I believe my wife does not know what to do with the money that is why the money remained there and she did not spend it before I was arrested. I paid one million into my wife account in UBA with the name Blessing Ogbewu – 2054098518.

NAMES AND ADDRESSES OF PROSECUTION WITNESSES
LIST OF PROSECUTION WITNESSES·

1. MOST. REV. IGNATIUS C.O. KATTEY
2. MRS. BEATRICE G. KATTEY
3. DR. LASISI ADEBUKOLA
4. IHEAKANWAH FELIX AZINZE
5. HONOURABLE FRED MBOMBO IGWE
6. DR. FIDELIS CHIGOZIE EZEM
7. CHIDIEBERE NWAWUBA
8. UKEL JEROME AGBA
9. HUMPHREY OHIKHUARE
10. REUBEN UZOMA
11. DESMOND ADAMU
12. FRIDAY EZEGBUNA

NAMES AND ADDRESSES OF ACCUSED PERSONS

1. CHIBUEZE NWAOGBA
   FEDERAL PRISON,
   PORT HARCOURT.

2. ONYEDIKACHI EMMANUEL OKORO
   FEDERAL PRISON,
   PORT HARCOURT.

3. PHILIP CHIKODIRI OGBUEWU
   FEDERAL PRISON,
   PORT HARCOURT.

22

183

I remember the fifties, when my father was a councillor. He took me with him when I was at an age not older than ten. A man had his money stolen, but he trusted his servant so much that he exonerated his servant. The magistrate asked the man why he thought his servant did not steal the money. The man said, 'He is an honest man. He did not steal the money.' The magistrate corrected him: 'You better say "As far as I know" or "To the best of my knowledge, my servant did not steal the money".'

It was this statement of the magistrate that stuck to my memory. Only God can be fully trusted when speaking about mortals, no matter how saintly he/she is. It is safer to say 'To the best of my knowledge . . .' or 'As far as I know . . .'

The Bible states clearly, with no apology:

> There is none righteous, no, not one. (Romans 3:10)

> For all have sinned and fallen short of the glory of God. (Romans 3:23)

> If we say we have no sin, we deceive ourselves, and the truth is not in us. If we confess our sin, He is faithful and just to forgive us our sins and to cleans us from all unrighteousness. If we say we have not sinned, we make Him a liar and His word is not in us. (1 John 1:8–10)

> Do not enter into judgment with Your servant, for in Your sight shall no man living be justified. (Psalm 143:2)

> If You O Lord should mark iniquity who shall stand? (Psalm 130:3)

God, speaking through the weeping prophet Jeremiah, said:

> The heart of man is deceitful above all things, and
> desperately wicked, who can know it.

> And God answers this question to give us hope

> I, the Lord, search the heart. I test the mind. Even
> to give every man according to his ways, according
> to the fruit of his doings. (Jeremiah 17:9–10)

We are not saying that you should trust no one, but rather, trust someone because you trust God. I always tell God to look at me through Jesus and never directly. If God looks at me directly, I am filthy, like a filthy rag. When one is saved through Jesus Christ, God sees that person through Jesus Christ.

I was called on to climb the witness box, which I did. My lawyer cross-examined me after I stated my name and did all the preliminary rituals that precede cross-examination.

Lawyer: You were kidnapped on 6 September 2013.

Response: Yes.

Lawyer: Can you recognise or identify those who kidnapped you?

Response: No. The kidnap took place at night, and for the days I was with them, they made sure I did not see their faces. [I think the lawyer was disappointed at this point.]

Lawyer: Can you tell the honourable court what happened from the time you were kidnapped together with your wife to the time of your release?

Response:	I have forgiven them. I forgave them and prayed for them the night I was released. I still have forgiven them.
Lawyer:	[shocked and disappointed] Just a little of the story of your kidnap.
Response:	The kidnap took place over five years ago. I am about seventy years old now. I don't think I want to go over all that happened and all that I went through. I have already forgiven them.
Lawyer:	Your Grace, why not let us know a brief . . .

At this point, the defendant's lawyers sought to bring my own lawyer to order. With the permission of the presiding judge, Justice Charles Wali, they insisted that it was wrong for my lawyer to persuade me to state my case.

(I have been told that kidnappers pay as much as between forty-five and seventy million naira (₦45,000,000–₦70,000,000), which is approximately equivalent to one hundred twenty-five to one hundred ninety-five thousand dollars ($125,000–$195,000), to their lawyers. This I cannot confirm.)

I was really surprised by the way the defendant lawyers were eager to defend my kidnappers. After my release, the Rivers State Director of the State Security Services invited me for an interview. During my ordeal, they were in contact with my family, and after my release, they wanted me to identify my kidnappers, though the kidnappers had confessed that they were responsible for my kidnap. According to the kidnappers, two of them died a few days after my kidnap. But the DSS told me a story that should be a lesson to all.

There was a kidnap case they were handling, and the lawyer was so aggressive in defending the kidnappers, perhaps because he had been paid so much money. One day, the lawyer came back to the

SSS and told them he was no longer interested in the case. The SSS asked him why. The lawyer told them that as he left the SSS and went home, *his own wife had been kidnapped.*

Kidnappers kidnapped the wife of the lawyer who was a defence counsel to kidnappers.

> Therefore, whatever you want men to do to you do also to them. For this is the law and the Prophets. (Matthew 7:12)

> Do not be deceived, God is not mocked, for whatever a man sows, that he will also reap. (Galatians 6:7)

Let us go back to the courtroom. As the lawyer of the defendants was busy defending the indefensible, my own lawyer continued— and rightly so—to urge me to state my own case, albeit briefly. The honourable judge cut in: 'The Archbishop says he is not ready and willing to go over the story of his ordeal. He said he has forgiven his kidnappers. There is no need to pressure him. He said he has forgiven them.'

The courtroom was dead silent. The judge then requested me to vacate the witness box. I heard some sort of giggling and rejoicing from the end of the accused, their hair shaved and they were shouting, 'Daddy, Daddy, Daddy, Daddy!'

To me, the kidnappers had insulted, despised, and challenged God by kidnapping me. They had seen me in my cassock, fully dressed, so they had not kidnapped me in error. It had been deliberate. What they did was a slap to God's face, and God knows how best to respond. When you fight a policeman on duty, you are fighting the president of the country; you are fighting the nation itself. The work of the police is to assist in bringing peace and order, and no matter how wrong he/she is, on duty he/she is representing the president, whose chief duty is security. My kidnappers were rejoicing that I had forgiven them, but God will still take over. I had forgiven them, but the government of the Federal Republic of Nigeria insisted on justice.

OTHER BOOKS BY THE AUTHOR INCLUDES:

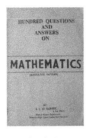

1) Hundred Questions and Answers on Mathematics

2) Foundation Mathematics

3) Ordination of Women: Give them a Chance

4) Handbook of Biblical Preaching

5) Family Psychology and Counselling

6) Handbook of Prayer

7) Order of Service for the Laying on of Hands and Anointing of the Sick

8) God Answers Prayer